ARCHITECTURAL REPRESENTATION

ARCHITECTURAL REPRESENTATION

Robert Greenstreet
James W. Shields
The University of Wisconsin-Milwaukee

PRENTICE HALL
Englewood Cliffs, New Jersey 07632

Library of Congress Cataloging-in-Publication Data

GREENSTREET, BOB.
Architectural representation.

Includes index.
1. Architectural drawing. 2. Architectural rendering. 3. Architecture—Designs and plans—Presentation drawings. 4. Architectural models.
I. Shields, James W. (date). II. Title.
NA2705.G74 1988 720'.284 87-1331
ISBN 0-13-044645-9

Editorial/production supervision: Reynold Rieger
Manufacturing buyers: Gordon Osbourne and Richard Washburn

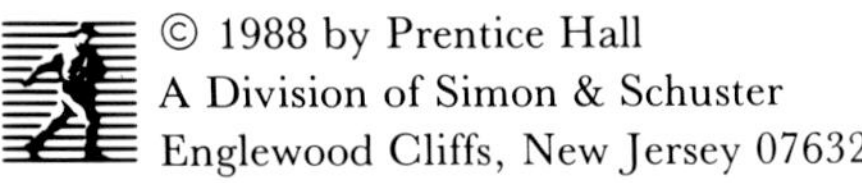

Printed in the United States of America

10 9 8 7 6 5 4 3 2 1

ISBN 0-13-044645-9 025

Prentice-Hall International (UK) Limited, *London*
Prentice-Hall of Australia Pty. Limited, *Sydney*
Prentice-Hall Canada Inc., *Toronto*
Prentice-Hall Hispanoamericana, S.A., *Mexico*
Prentice-Hall of India Private Limited, *New Delhi*
Prentice-Hall of Japan, Inc., *Tokyo*
Simon & Schuster Asia Pte. Ltd., *Singapore*
Editora Prentice-Hall do Brasil, Ltda., *Rio de Janeiro*

Contents

Preface

There are numerous books in print concerning architectural graphics. Most deal with the technical aspects involved in the achievement of certain graphic effects and show examples of work that may be emulated or even traced. However, few of these texts try to explore the implications of using particular kinds of graphics in the design process or comment upon the applicability of certain techniques to the range of projects that may be undertaken. Certainly, it is rare to find any form of historical background to a particular technique, illustrating its original intended impact and method of application. Thus, in some cases, it can be observed that graphics are used either inappropriately or inexpertly, not solely in the presentation process where they may affect the audience's opinion and perception of the project, but also in the design process where misapplied techniques may affect the designer's handling of the project.

The primary purpose of this book, therefore, is to explore in detail some of the more important and useful graphic devices that will help the designer in thinking about the illustration of space and form. The contents are not designed to be comprehensive in their coverage of graphic techniques, but seek instead to represent selectively those which are potentially the most effective in presentation and which can give the designer the greatest understanding and insight during the process of design. For this purpose, several well-known techniques are extensively illustrated to show their development and appropriate application. In addition, some recently developed techniques are described, as well as several little known graphic conventions which, despite their antiquity or relative obscurity, provide some invaluable insights into the understanding of space and form, and the effective communication of the results to the intended audience.

The authors would like to thank the faculty, students, and alumni of the Department of Architecture, The University of Wisconsin-Milwaukee, for providing some of the illustrations that supplement the text.

ROBERT GREENSTREET
JAMES W. SHIELDS

Milwaukee, Wisconsin

Illustration Acknowledgments

Many of the illustrations in this book have been undertaken by students, alumni, or faculty of The School of Architecture and Urban Planning, The University of Wisconsin-Milwaukee. They include:

Name	*Figure(s)*
Beckley/Myers, Inc., Architects	3.22
K. Christian	7.16
K. Forseth	7.19, 7.20, 7.21
S. Greiczek	2.2, 2.9
J. Highum	3.17
R. Hoffman	3.25, 7.18
J. Huberty	7.2, 7.3
D. Jaeckels	4.9
D. Jennerjahn	2.7, 2.14, 2.15, 7.5
M. Klancic	7.5, 7.7
K. Kemp	5.10
R. Locast	3.15, 5.2
M. Martin	6.7
G. Mascari	7.11
G. Meyer	7.13, 7.14
P. Murphy	6.17
F. Nourzad	7.6
J. Peot	Chapter 7 opening, 7.4
G. Randall	7.6
D. Reed	6.8, 7.12
C. Riesterer	1.29, 2.1, 7.5
T. Hausmann	7.10
A. Schnarsky, Associate Professor	3.26
C. Thiel	6.11
R. Van Gilder	3.24
W. Weissmann	7.17
D. Wickwire	7.15
J. Zapala	6.10

Thanks are also due to Steve McEnroe who undertook all the photography in Chapter Six.

Figures 1.1 and 1.4 are reproduced from *The Four Books of Architecture* by Andrea Palladio, originally edited and published by Isaac Ware in 1738, and published by Dover Publications, Inc. in 1965.

ARCHITECTURAL REPRESENTATION

Introduction

Graphic representation can serve a number of roles in relation to architectural design. The most obvious is the clarification and communication of ideas and intentions from the designer to a client or, eventually, to a contractor. In these roles the purpose, and therefore the nature, of the graphic product is different. Drawings for clients, for example, are intended not merely to communicate but also to persuade, convince, or impress. Communications to contractors need only transmit detailed technical information to ensure the correct construction of the project. Obviously, the graphic techniques used for these two purposes are likely to be different, and misuse in either case could lead to confusion or misunderstanding.

However, graphic application goes beyond the basic communication of information to known parties. Competition entries, for example, are intended for general display and may be adjudicated by a group of individuals unknown to the designer. Here the designer has no opportunity for verbal explanation and has no way to accurately assess the level at which the presentation of the scheme should be targeted. The choice of graphic style is therefore most important to ensure adequate communication of the ideas inherent in the scheme.

Drawing and related techniques are fundamental not only to the generation of individual schemes, but to the larger development of design ideas within the profession. It is therefore important to view the role of graphics, particularly drawing, not solely as a series of image-making techniques, but in the light of its relevance to the advancement of architectural thought.

It could be argued that the relationship between a drawing and the design it depicts is primarily one of subordination, the drawing being merely a means to the completion of the final product. However, this assessment tends to undervalue the significance of drawing in the generation of images, where traditionally architects and designers have utilized techniques of delineation as the primary tools of design. Since these techniques carry with them certain consequences that affect the way in which space and form are perceived, understood, and manipulated, the type of drawing used by the designer may affect the outcome of the design and therefore the final, buildable solution. Thus, drawing can be regarded as an important and influential factor in the design process. This assessment raises questions about the appropriateness of certain techniques to some design problems. For example, if the drawing type is inappropriate to the problem or has been selected out of fashionable preference or whim, it is possible that the vehicle of delineation may adversely affect the designer's thinking by the depiction of spaces and forms in a particular way, and therefore impact upon the final solution.

In the generation of new ideas, the drawing can be regarded as a tool of primary importance. In recent years the drawings generated by architects to communicate their work have become the focus of much attention and several major exhibitions and publications.[1] They have transcended the role of the simple blueprint to become artworks in their own right; drawings—at least those by more prominent architects—are exhibited for sale in art galleries, commanding considerable prices, and are the focus, fulcrum, and vehicle for many debates within the profession.[2] The drawing here becomes not merely a medium of communication, but a tangible product which, regardless of any form or space which it may subsequently generate, is conceived as a vehicle of dissemination of design ideas perhaps even more powerful than the built form itself. Compared to the freedom of painting or sculpture, for example, architecture is an art of patience, deliberation, and confinement, and major projects can often take years from initial development to their final execution. The whim of clients, zoning commissions, and bankers can control the nature of a project and shape its forms as effectively as a sculptor shapes a piece of clay.

Sir John Summerson wrote that "architecture is a chained and fettered art . . . but when once we remove architecture from the arena of the solid and material . . . we are free at last to depict those things which architecture might do in certain circumstances. . . ." Critical to this statement is the phrase "to depict." Architects typically have turned to drawings, rather than models, the written word, or other media, when they want to communicate their visions of the future. Liberated from the constraints of clients, law, or finance, architects have used drawings to shape the nature of thought in the profession. When Neoclassicism was the preeminent style in Europe, it was not so much the buildings of classical antiquity themselves that had caused its rise in popularity, but the drawings by Piranesi (and others), which had shown both the profession and public a vision of architecture so powerful that they helped to change the face of nearly every European city.[3] However, Piranesi's "Vedute di Roma" were not merely pictorial images of antiquity; they were also ideological propaganda. The architect favored Roman rather than Greek architecture, and his drawings were intended largely to promote the use of Roman forms in new designs. It was thus the power of drawings, with their ability to alter, magnify, and convince, that allowed Piranesi to promote his ideologies effectively.[4]

More recently, when Le Corbusier attempted to establish his vision of the modern city, he achieved it, not with a built commission, but with drawings. These graphic works, published and widely disseminated, depicted Corbusier's visualization of the new world as real and inevitable, and showed the city of the past as outdated and harmful. There was no client or budget in these designs. In fact, given the scope of his proposed architectural and social reform, these things were largely irrelevant.[5] There was even, in the case of his 1920s projects for Paris, probably no serious intent of execution. The crystal towers, drawn floating above the green ruins of Paris, could epitomize the idea of the new age as no "real" project ever could. The drawings thus had asserted themselves as a reality independent of the built world, the effect of which has been profound: few major cities in the world today exist without some legacy of Le Corbusier's influence.

Even today, when architects with visionary tendencies seek to influence contemporary architectural thought, they turn not to practice, but to drawing and publication. Leon Krier, for example, without a single constructed building to his credit, has ascended to a position of international prominence and influence based entirely upon his drawings.[6] In less extreme cases, architects such as Michael Graves became influential pioneers in architectural design at a time when they may have had only a handful of small commissions completed. These architects generate drawings of beauty and skill which have the ability to epitomize their ideologies better than actual buildings, limited as the latter are by the confines of budget and reality.

Despite their use as a vehicle for higher theoretical debate, however, visionary drawings have perhaps more direct application to "mainstream" education and practice.[7] The British architect Phillip Tilden stated that "it is essential for every artist, as he works at his own problem at hand, to occupy himself also with some scheme of magnitude. It matters not whether his castle or cathedral be on paper, and never reach . . . realization. . . . He will be building up his own character and ideals in the process."

The suggestion here is that architects can use the visionary drawing as an exercise to clarify and intensify their architectural ideas. Working without the constraints of the client, program, or budget can allow a designer to fully develop architectural ideas which might normally be excluded or diluted. These clarified and supposedly pure ideas might then be reapplied to some degree to subsequent real commissions. Competitions, which by their initially theoretical nature may be seen as visionary opportunities, have often served in this role. Regarding competitions as an expressive and creative outlet rather than as a service rendered has allowed architectural drawing to become the vehicle for some of the major developments in design as, for example, in the case of the Houses of Parliament in London—the object of a major theoretical battle of styles in the nineteenth century.

Thus, drawings can be regarded as a powerful, influential, and integral element in the development of architectural thought and design, although, as previously suggested, the drawing types to be used must be considered carefully. If a particular drawing convention affects in some way the user's perception of space and form, it will ultimately impact upon the design and any debate thereby generated. Consequently, it is important for the designer to be fully aware of the available range of drawing types, their effects, applications, and appropriateness to certain projects to ensure a compatible match between the tool and product, thereby maximizing the potential for a successful outcome to the scheme.

It is reasonable to assume that some specific drawing types have become associated with certain architectural ideas. In this way, they may even be considered symbolic forms, where a particular ideological thrust becomes connected with a tangible form or symbol and is thereby intimately associated with it. The figure ground plan is a good example of such a symbolic form, a drawing type closely associated with formalist urban design and the configuration of spaces as contained and defined figures.[8] It is the extensive use and publication of figure ground drawings by the proponents of these ideologies (Leon Krier, O. M. Ungers, and Colin Rowe, for example) that has resulted in this close formal association. All of this is predicated on the understanding that certain kinds of drawings have unique and specific characteristics which have suggested their application to certain problems.

As architectural ideologies shift and change, it can be argued that specific drawing types will become identified with new architectural points of view. During the 1920s, for example, perspective drawing was seen by many to contradict modern artists' and architects' conception of space, and many designers no longer felt that perspective techniques corresponded "to the objective and unequivocal representation of space" but rather that they "rendered space limited, finite, and closed."[9] In contrast, axonometric and oblique drawings were seen as uniquely suited to modern use and theory. Theo van Doesburg, for instance, stressed the suitability of axonometrics to the design of the new "spatial architecture." He wrote that

> the new principle of a spatial and functional architecture designed by the axonometrical method has already been demonstrated. This kind of representation permits the simultaneous perception of each part of the house, seen in its correct proportions, that is without the vanishing points of perspective. . . .[10]

In this way, the paraline drawing as well as the perspective both became attitudinally fixed in their symbolic relationship to style and were used accordingly. While the specific meaning of drawing types will continue to change as architectural ideologies change, it is perhaps most significant that architects have seen certain kinds of drawings as ideally suited to certain tasks, while they have viewed others as diametrically opposed to their efforts.

If, however, a drawing type is selected on the basis of stylistic preference rather than compatibility with the problem at hand, the result may be a questionable coupling of technique and design scheme. A simple example would be the design and depiction of a single-story, flat-roofed building of considerable square footage using the currently popular technique of oblique projection. Although in many cases it is a useful design and presentation tool, the oblique, by virtue of its configuration, will show the roof of the building in its entirety, while distorting and limiting visual access to the facades below. Not only does this drawing convey to an audience an imbalance of information (unless, of course, there is some important reason for the choice, such as the incorporation of a roof garden, for example, viewed from a taller neighboring building), it suggests that if the designer used the drawing type in the generation of the design, a similar distortion of understanding may have taken place, perhaps limiting the designer's ability to provide the optimum solution. Furthermore, ideological preference may not be the only factor which influences the choice of drawing type; simple habit or a tendency to select on the basis of ease of application rather than appropriateness to the specific task may also affect the final outcome of the design.

This introductory chapter has sought to explore the nature of architectural graphics and the importance of its relationship to design. It has attempted to highlight some of the problems inherent in the use of graphic techniques and to identify the impact this may have on design. In addition, it has addressed the inappropriate use or inadequate application of certain drawing types in the design and presentation processes.

The purpose of the first three chapters in Section One of this book, therefore, is to explore in detail the range of drawing types available to the designer and to comment upon their appropriate use and application. The remaining chapters in Section Two explore a number of techniques that may be effective in the design and presentation processes, both in their ability to clarify spatial understanding and to enable fast, effective application and communication. Although many of the drawing types are likely to be generated by basic pen or pencil techniques onto various translucent or opaque surfaces, they have, it was felt, been exhaustively explored in many other graphic texts. Accordingly, they are not repeated in this book to enable more detailed consideration to be given to techniques less adequately covered elsewhere.

It is hoped that, in total, the contents of the book will provide the reader with a comprehensive understanding of the appropriate uses of major drawing types as well as outlining sufficient practical information to ensure their successful completion.

1. A. Drexler, *The Architecture of the Ecole des Beaux-Arts.* Massachusetts Institute of Technology, 1977. An example of both a book and an influential exhibition.
2. R. Banham, *Iso! Axo! (All Fall Down?).* North Carolina School of Design Publication, 1978. Contains some pointed remarks concerning "gallery" architecture.
3. A. P. Gomez, *Architecture and the Crisis of Modern Science.* Massachusetts Institute of Technology, 1983, pp. 257–258.

4. R. S. Johnson, *Piranesi, Master of Graphic Art.* Chicago, 1980. Provides a discussion of Piranesi's drawings and influence.
5. Le Corbusier, *The Ville Radieuse.* Paris, 1935.
6. D. Pophyrios, *Leon Krier, Houses, Places, Cities.* Architectural Design Profile, 1984.
7. J. Lever and M. Richardson, *The Architect as Artist.* New York, 1984. Gives a brief outline of "paper architecture" and visionary work contained in the collection of the Royal Institute of British Architects.
8. W. Copper, "The Figure Grounds," *Cornell Journal of Architecture,* Fall 1983, pp. 42-53.
9. B. Reichlin, "The Axonometric as Project." *Lotus International,* No. 22.
10. *Ibid.*, p. 85.

Section One

DRAWING TYPES

Chapter One

Plan, Section, and Elevation Drawing

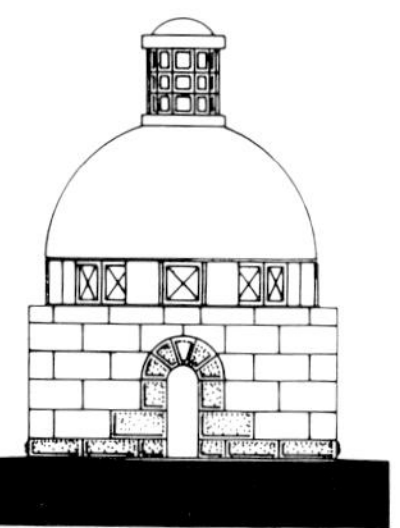

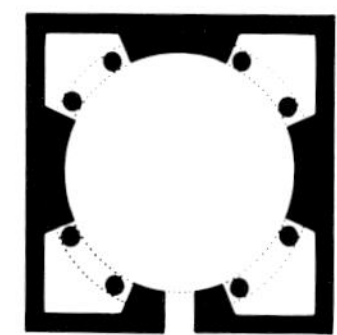

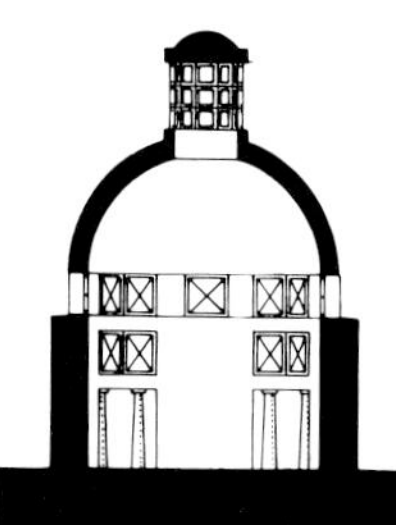

Orthographic projection—specifically the use of the plan, section, and elevation—is perhaps the most commonly used convention in architecture. By disassembly of a three-dimensional form into two-dimensional "slices," various aspects of the design can be accurately, although separately, displayed. It is used most commonly in the production of construction documents, where the need for exact, measurable information overrides that for spatial or qualitative character. The lack of such character may be considered to limit the use of orthographic drawings in the design and presentation processes. However, the plan, elevation, and section do have the capacity to be qualitatively rather than technically oriented and can be used in the depiction of spatial information. The weakness of orthographic drawing types in illustrating a single space with several discrete images can be overcome with a number of interesting techniques, some of them little known to architects. The following subsections seek to explore the potential of the plan, section, and elevation in the design and presentation processes.

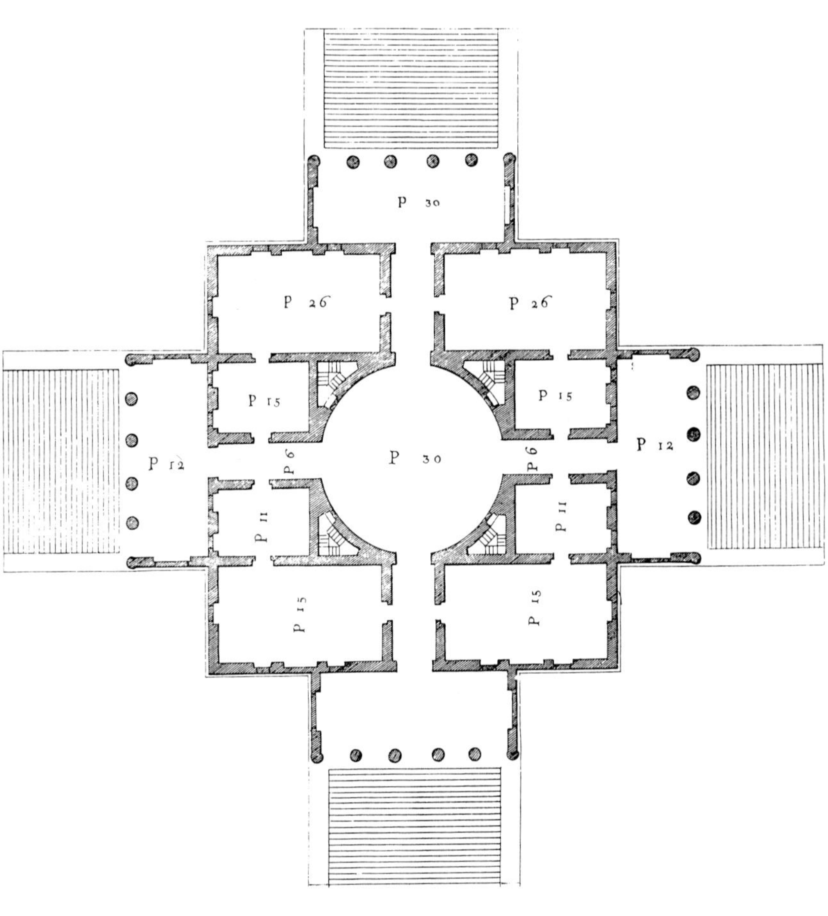

Figure 1.1
Plan of the Villa Rotunda, from Palladio's "Four Books."

THE PLAN

One of the better-known architectural aphorisms of the twentieth century is Le Corbusier's "The plan is the generator." Employed throughout the design process from the earliest conceptual stage, the plan view has inherent characteristics both positive and negative which can color, alter, and control the designer's perceptions of form and space. However, although ostensibly plan drawings are a simple and direct means of depiction, familiarity with their conventions can conceal their inherent abstraction. Consider for a moment what a plan view of a building really represents: a building, generally an imaginary one, shorn off above a floor plane (usually at a height of three feet above ground level), as seen from above (but simultaneously above any given point), and projected onto a flat sheet of paper. Although this is an extreme description, it illustrates that plans are in fact an abstraction which occur in a medium impossible to experience in the built world.

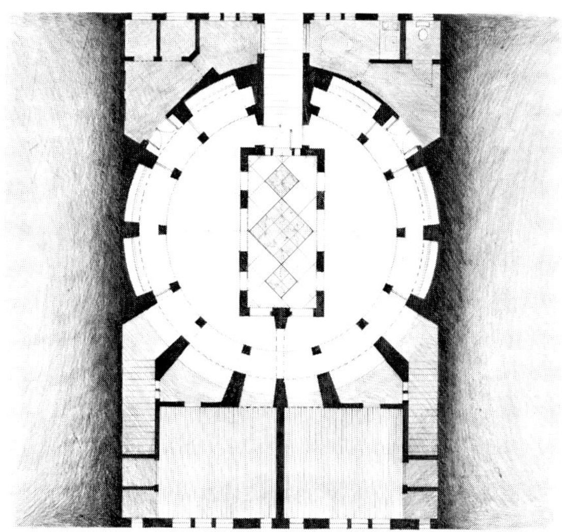

Figure 1.2
Sketch plan of a retail renovation project, featuring a skylit atrium which sits within a large round room. The concept and geometric order were first conceived and recorded in the plan view, representing the design procedures typically employed by architects.

PROBLEMS WITH THE PLAN

Designing with an abstract system like the plan can raise questions and create problems which are not immediately apparent. Among them is the novice designer's belief that the plan is primarily the most important generator of a design. Educators often are told by a student: "I'll do the sections and elevations when I'm done with the plan." Obviously, this attitude can lead to poorly developed designs. It is fair to assume that many professionals, too, continue to see the plan as the primary, and often singular, design tool.

THE FLAT SURFACE

Perhaps the greatest difficulty that designers experience is their tendency to resolve a plan as a flat graphic pattern rather than as a drawing of a three-dimensional building. In this way, major organizational concepts can be developed which seem logical from the plan viewpoint, but which in fact may be relatively indecipherable, or cannot be experienced in a real building. An example of such a phenomenon can be seen in Ledoux's plan for a House of Pleasure at the ideal city of Chaux, which takes on the overall pattern of a phallus, visible only in plan. This illustrates how designers can use plans to design drawings instead of using them to design buildings. In Ledoux's case, this may have been intentional, although the problem with this approach is apparent in many buildings that are eventually built. Take, for example, any number of formal, axial buildings which have attempted to conform to the rigors of the plan by balancing noncompatible functions in equally sized and shaped spaces, primarily in the interests of an axial balancing which in most cases can be perceived *only* in the plan drawing.

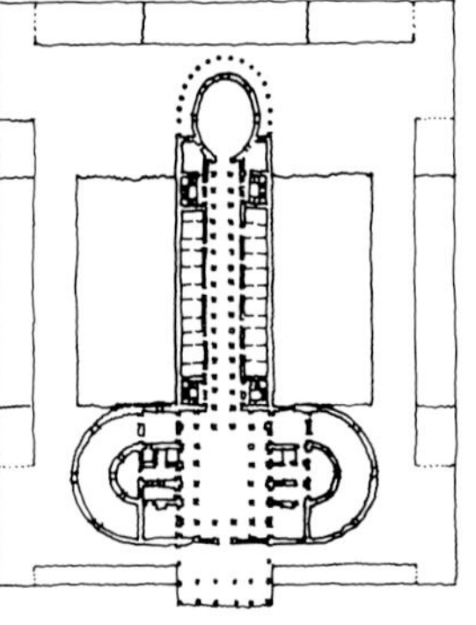

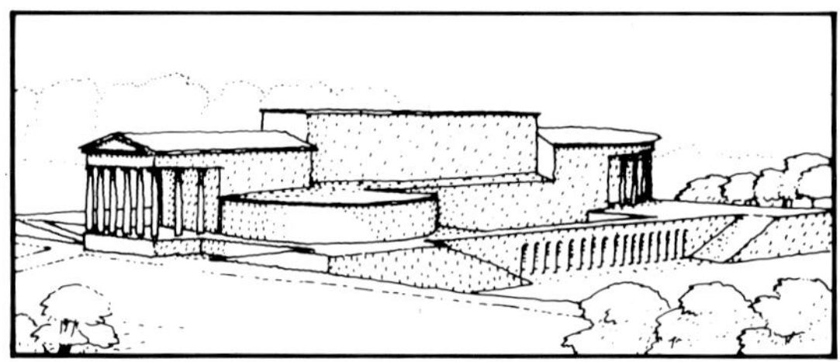

Figure 1.3
Plan and perspective views of C. N. Ledoux's House of Pleasure. The symbolic intentions which order and shape the plan are virtually unrecognizable in the perspective view.

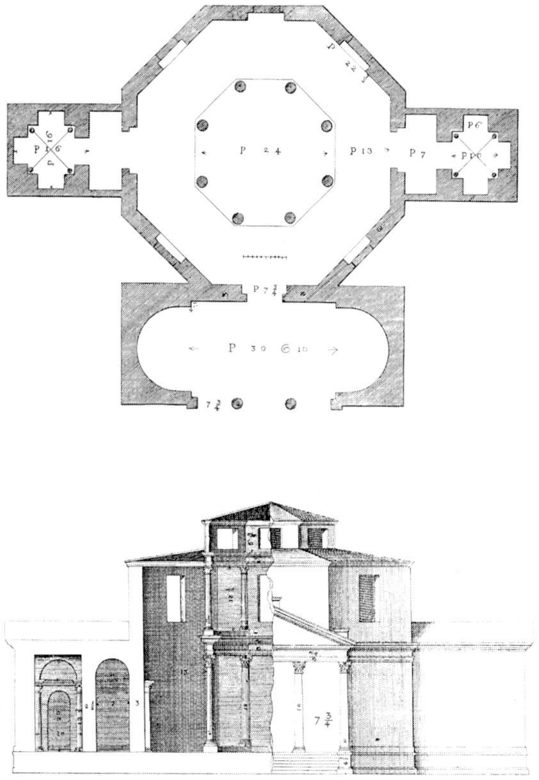

LOSS OF COMMUNICATIVE POWER

The twentieth century has seen a critical loss of communicative power in the plan. In the past, load-bearing masonry construction developed into a limited and distinct series of spatial types, such as barrel vaults, domes, groins, coffered ceilings, and porticos. Each of these spatial types had more or less distinct planometric configurations which were widely used and recognizable. For example, a domed space was generally round or square (with pendentives), while the walls surrounding the space were thicker than normal to support the increased loading. When drawn in plan, this configuration could be viewed as a spatial volume, even when not associated with a section or elevation. Such conventions allowed designers to use and develop plans for which the three-dimensional implications were immediately apparent.

This situation has been changed by the advent of modern frame construction. The thickness of a curtain wall for a fifty-story tower need not differ from that of a curtain wall for a one-story structure, whether it be of glass or of stone veneer. Furthermore, since most rooms are contained by non-load-bearing walls, they can assume any number of configurations. Thus, the previously accepted distinct spatial types have become largely redundant, and it is now possible to look at a plan and gain little or no understanding of the corresponding volumes of space above.

This has limited the usefulness of the plan as a design tool, which may not adequately explore space if not used in conjunction with other drawing types. Some of the following techniques may be useful in minimizing the problems of designing with the plan and ensuring that it is used to its full potential in the design process.

Figure 1.4
This drawing of a temple reveals a direct and intimate relationship between the plan and its three-dimensional form. Even without association to the corresponding section elevation, the plan can be read spatially.

POCHÉ AND THE FIGURE GROUND

The figure ground drawing is an invaluable tool for the designer, and poché (that is, the technique of coloring or filling in between lines) is the means by which such drawings are accomplished. Its enabling the viewer to clearly discriminate built, solid form from unbuilt void is the value of this drawing type, and its use instead of simple line drawings can have a powerful impact upon the designs produced. Initially, one might expect that the shapes of wall, piers, and columns should appear as black "figures" against the white "ground" of the paper. However, the traditional use of poché and the figure ground is in fact the opposite, whereby the built solid as "ground" is configured around the unbuilt void, which will be contained and perceived as "figure." The notion of space as "figural volumes" has been widely used in the past, and it is only in this century that designers have neglected its use as a principal design model.

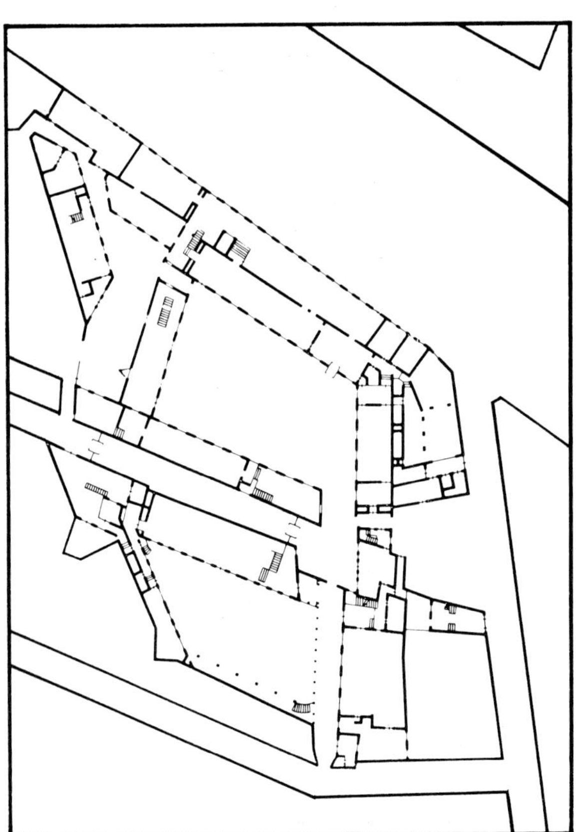

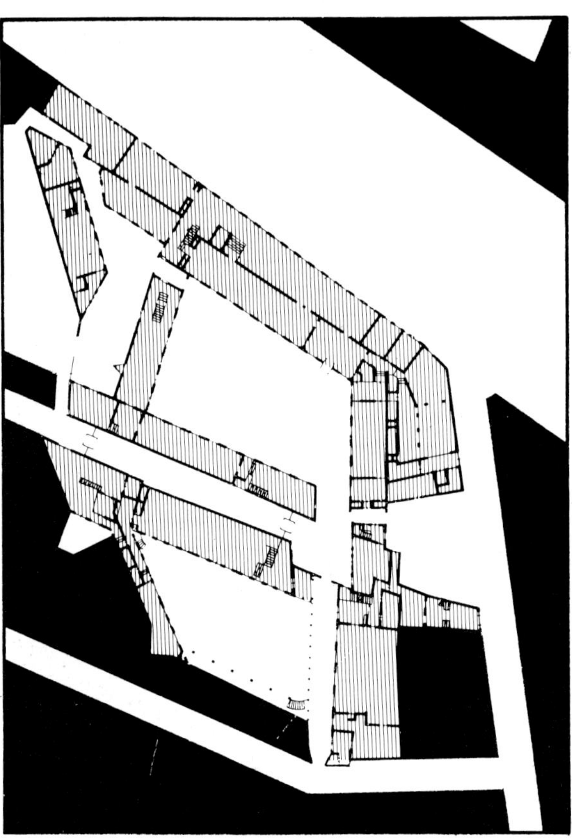

Figure 1.5
These comparative drawings of Amsterdam's Historische Museum show the significance of poché. The line drawing is confusing and spatially ambiguous, while the pochéd version clearly illustrates the museum's system of courts and passageways.

THE FIGURE GROUND IN URBAN DESIGN

Figure ground drawings are perhaps most typically employed in urban design projects, allowing the designer to perceive the shapes of buildings clearly and, as importantly, the resultant configurations of streets, squares, courtyards, and spaces that constitute the city. To situate new buildings with sensitivity, to design volumes of space in an existing context, or indeed to undertake any kind of urban design scheme, a figure ground plan of the existing context is highly desirable. Several different types of figure ground configurations are available for these kinds of design problems.

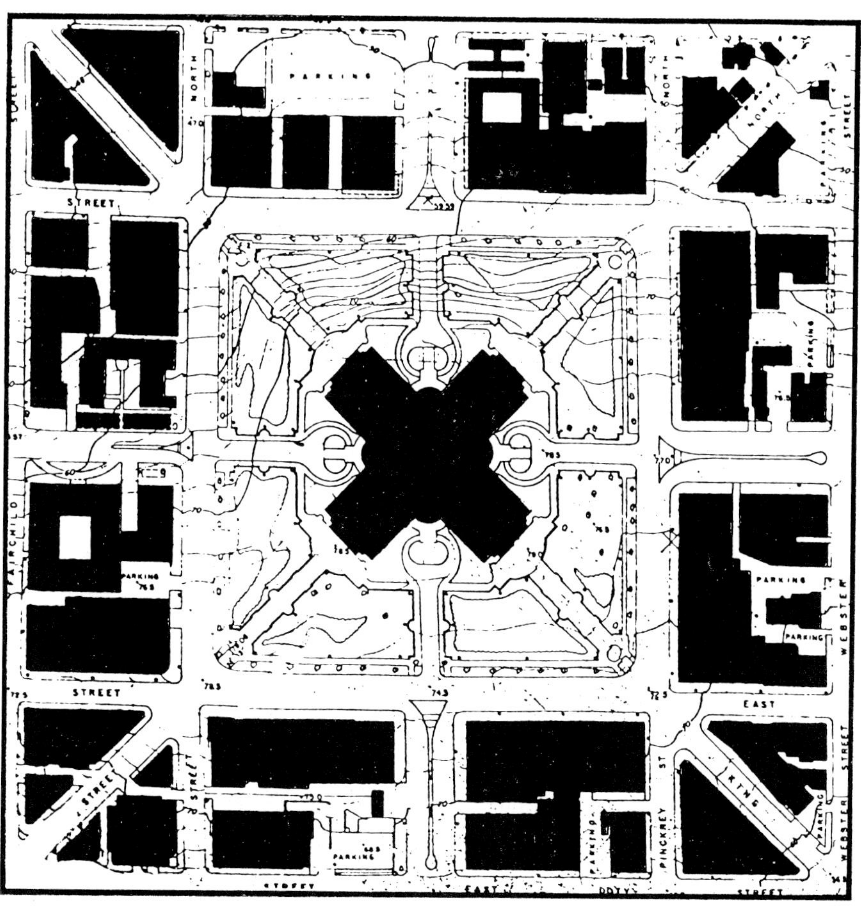

Figure 1.6
Partial plan of Madison, Wisconsin, with streets radiating from the State Capitol building. With the use of heavy poché, the drawing clearly describes the central square as a figure of enclosed space dominated by the diagonally sited Capitol. Curbs, walks, and major trees are all shown in light lines.

Figure 1.7
The irregular urban fabric of central Boston is revealed in the figure ground with a clarity not possible with simple line drawings.

CONTEXTUAL FIGURE GROUNDS

Contextual urban plans are often handled as figure grounds and are best used when the area under design consideration has many existing buildings and connections to the city fabric. These drawings should generally be prepared early in the design process so that they can be used when initial concepts are being developed. Producing sketches as tracing overlays on a contextual figure ground can have a powerful effect on the kind of schemes developed.

Basic building configurations can be studied effectively in a contextual figure ground drawing, especially when the project is sited in an urban context. Shape, setbacks, building thickness, contextual fit, and spatial formations can be seen clearly when drawn with high contrast. Scales are generally chosen that allow a large portion of the surrounding area to be seen. Furthermore, smaller drawings are faster in execution, which should encourage multiple iterations early in the design stage. When designing a site plan that shows a broader context, concepts and possibilities often become apparent which would otherwise be lost if the building were studied in abstract isolation. It is sometimes useful to give the context one tone and the design itself a darker one, perhaps in double hatching or in black. This technique not only shows the basic building outline but allows courtyards, atria, or major interior spaces to be left in white, giving them a prominent quality in the drawing.

REVERSE FIGURE GROUND

Reverse figure ground drawings are sometimes used by designers, where the built form is represented in white and resultant spaces receive poché in black or dark tone. This drawing type is generally employed in urban designs because it is felt that the spaces, receiving the dark emphasis usually reserved for built form, are perceived more intensely and as such receive more design attention than in traditionally rendered drawings. Typically, architects work by making dark marks on a white sheet. This process can lead to the idea that the things drawn, the "dark marks" (usually built solids), are hierarchically the most important, and the resultant spaces are secondary. The reverse figure ground can be used in the design process to change this perception so that volumes of space are drawn as figures and the built solids are left as residual. This provides an alternative viewpoint by reemphasizing the spatial content of the design problem.

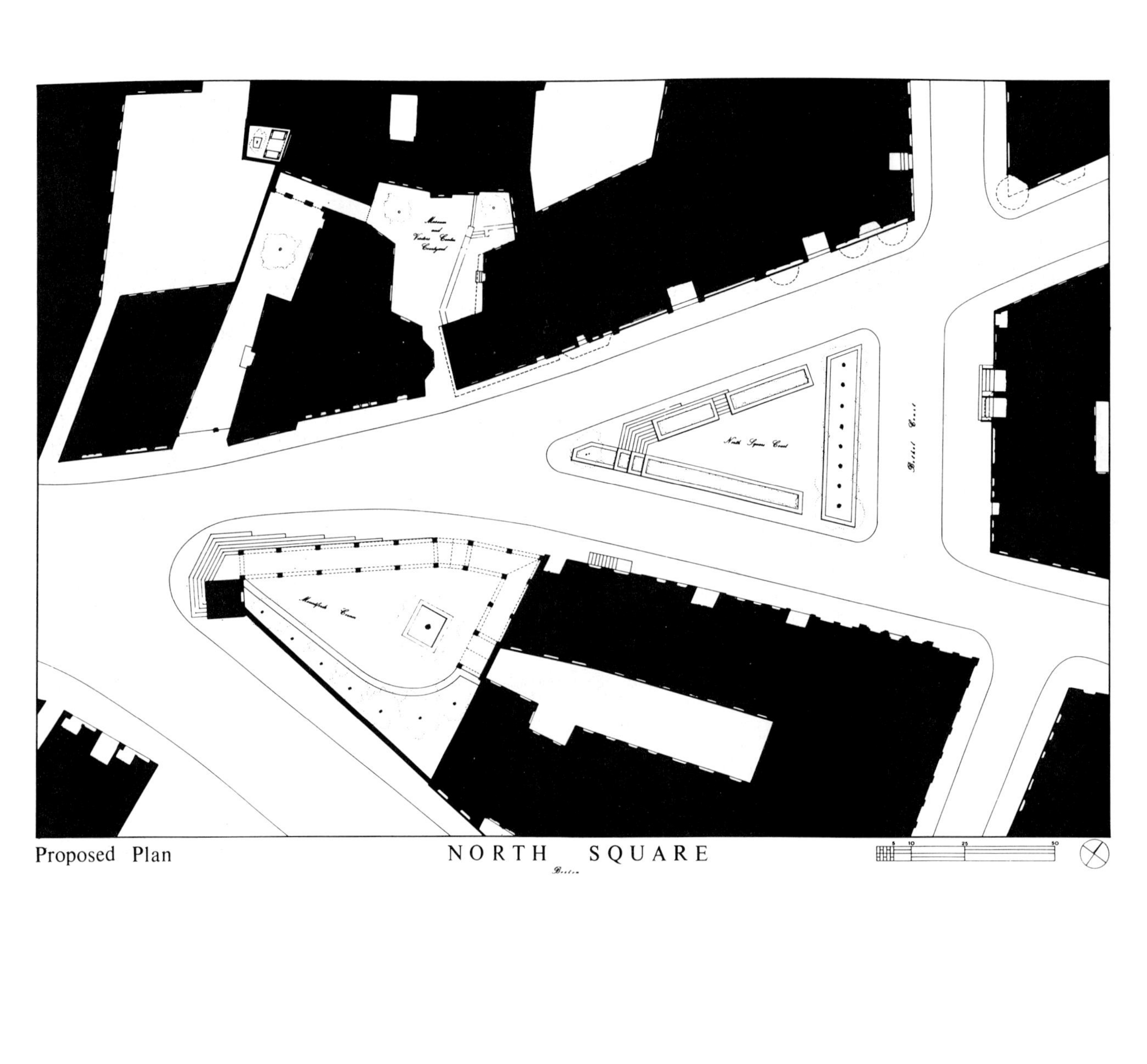

Figure 1.8
An urban design scheme for Boston's North Square is shown in figure ground, with entourage drawn in fine lines. As in most figure grounds, no building plans are shown.

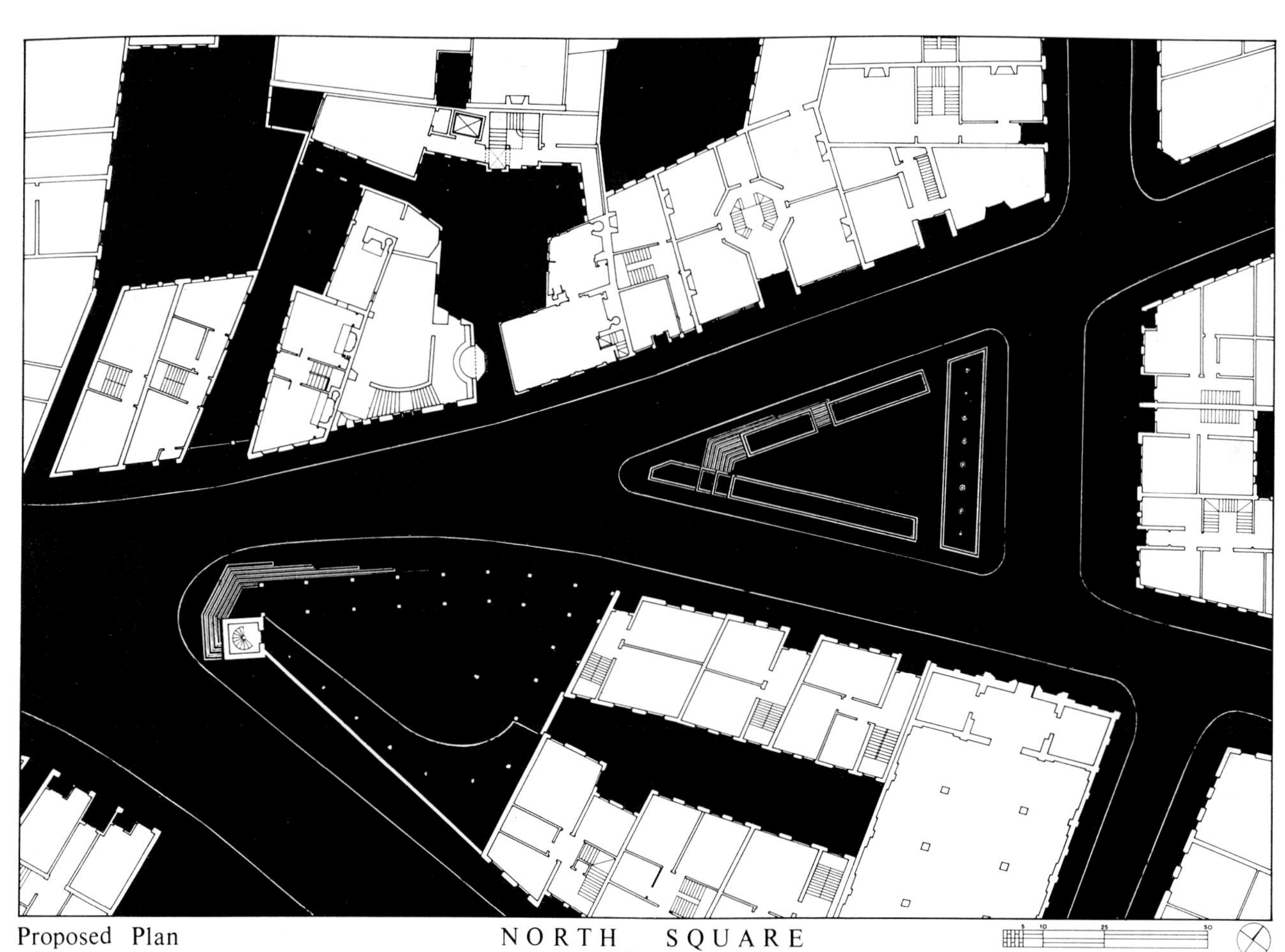

Figure 1.9
Reverse figure ground of North Square, in which all open spaces receive black poché. All building plans can be revealed as line drawings, while curbs, steps, and other entourage can be described with fine white lines.

ENTOURAGE

Entourage drawings are in some ways similar to reverse figure grounds. The term *entourage* refers primarily to landscape elements, paving texture, vegetation, and architectural features which can be drawn so as to produce an overall tone on the ground plane, leaving building shapes in white. Shadows are often used to enhance the effect. This manner of drawing has some of the advantages of the reverse figure ground but usually takes much more time to prepare. It is therefore used more often in the later, more detailed stages of the design process and can become an effective device in the final presentation of the completed scheme.

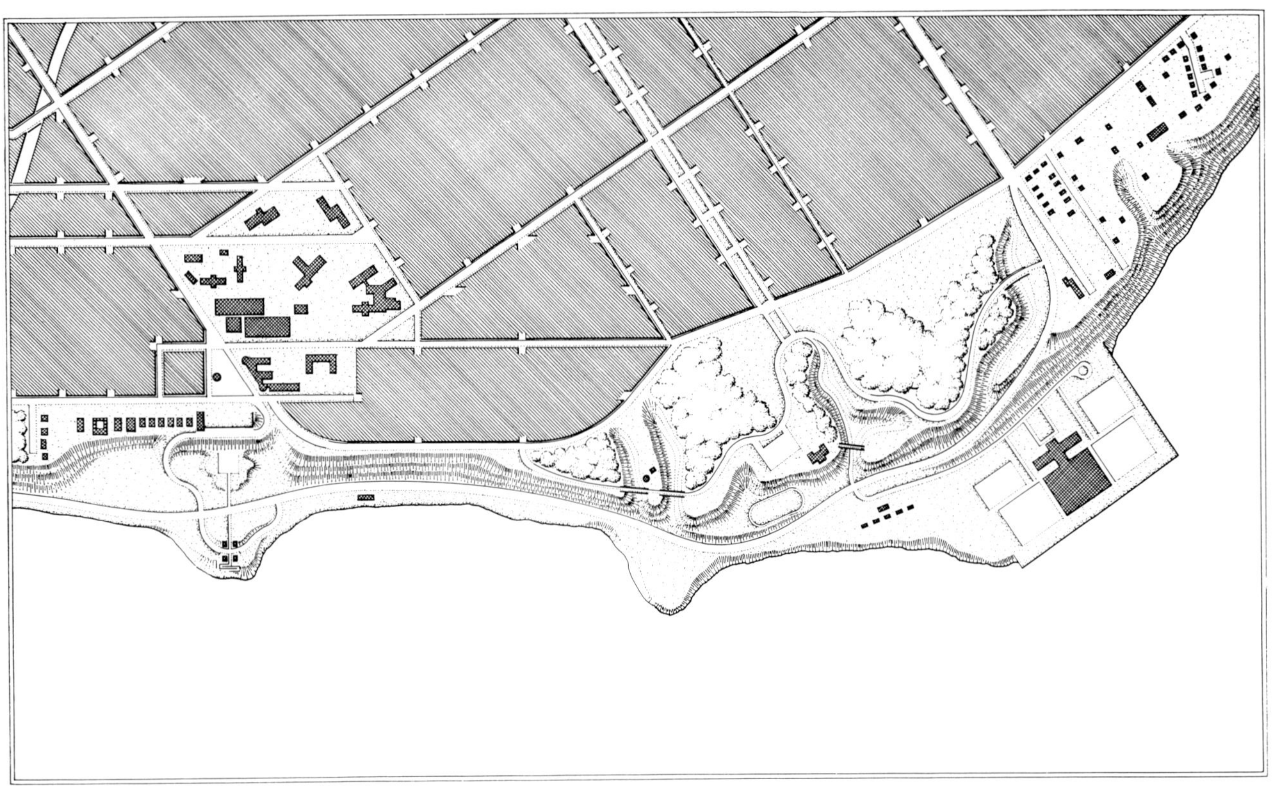

Figure 1.10
Scheme for Milwaukee's Watertower Park is drawn in the context of the entire lakefront district, allowing the designer to deal with urban design issues which might have been otherwise ignored.

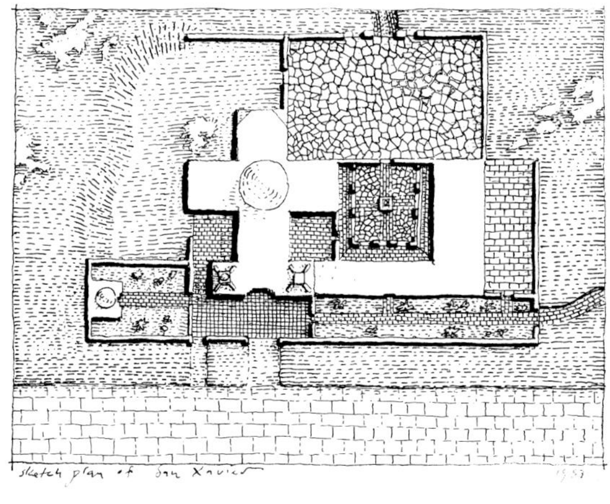

Figure 1.11
Entourage elements are rendered so as to produce an overall ground plan tone in this sketch of San Xavier Mission near Tucson, Arizona. The technique, similar in many ways to a reverse figure ground, directs attention (of both designer and observer) toward the shape and texture of outdoor spaces.

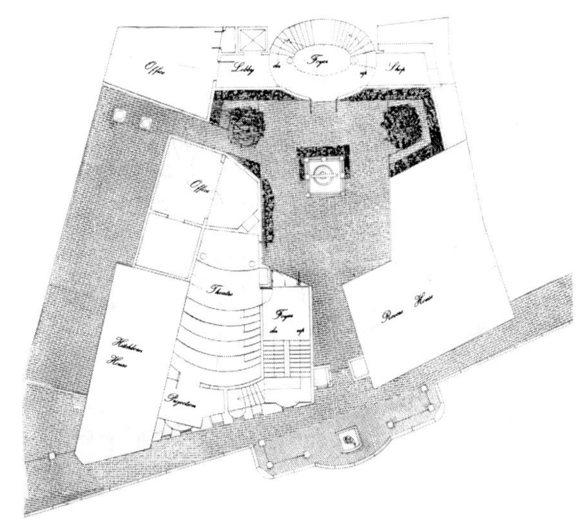

Figure 1.12
A proposal for a museum addition to Paul Revere's house in Boston was envisioned as a series of figural outdoor rooms, which are rendered with the texture of brick pavers. The drawing places emphasis on the shapes (or figures) of the courtyards and treats the enclosing built solids as white ground.

STUDY OF PUBLIC SPACE

When a point in the design process has been reached where the basic configuration of interior spaces has been determined, it is sometimes useful to hatch (or poché) the minor or service spaces of a building to enable major public spaces to emerge as dominant figures. In a design for a major hotel, for example, kitchens, storage and service areas, and other private rooms would receive poché. The lobby, atrium, banquet hall, and other important public spaces would then remain white, in the way streets and squares in an urban figure ground would be presented. In this way, their shapes and interconnections can be studied further without the visual distraction of the secondary spaces.

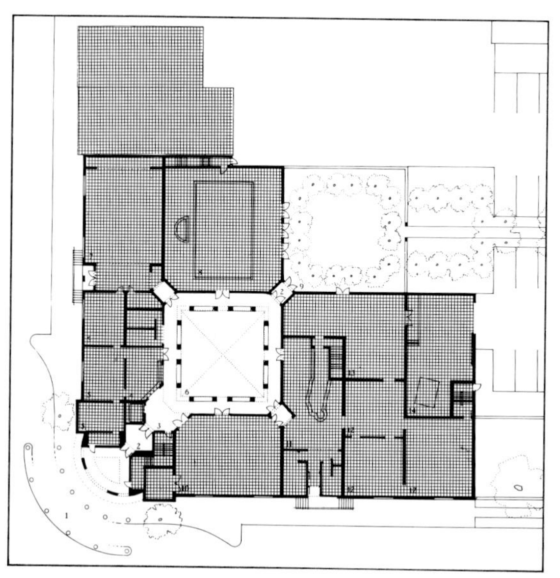

Figure 1.13
The shape of a public atrium in a resort-town hotel is clearly seen when surrounding secondary spaces receive a grey tone. Reminiscent of the famous Nolli plan of Rome, this drawing type depicts built solids as poché which contain the public realm, while allowing the detailed plan to be revealed.

USE OF MOSAIQUE

Mosaique was a term used at the Ecole des Beaux-Arts, referring to the design and rendering of the ground floor plane in a way that allows built solids to remain white, while toned floor planes recede in depth. Although these kinds of drawings can sometimes be used for sketch designing, they generally take so long to complete that they are more typically used in presentation work. The pattern of stone, brick, or tile (hence mosaique) joints can also be correlated to a reflected ceiling plan, allowing the designer a broader range of information with which to work on the various surfaces of the design.

Figure 1.14
This mosaique plan shows every joint in a two-tone marble floor. The pattern of joints corresponds to the positions of beams, joists, coffers, and central oculus above, allowing the plan to describe the nature of the space without becoming a true reflected ceiling plan.

BUILDING DESIGN AND CONVENTIONAL PLANS

A number of drawing conventions can be used in the handling of building plans, and their speed of execution, usefulness as design tools, and communicative potential varies widely. The same design, drawn in different ways, can appear substantially different, which suggests that the kind of drawing used changes the way that designers work and perhaps alters their perceptions of design. The various way in which plans are typically handled can be broken down into three basic categories; line drawings, poché, and plan shadowing.

Line Drawings

Line drawings represent the most typical approach to plans, each wall or built solid being described by two lines. This is generally accepted as the simplest and, for most designers, fastest system for plans, although it has major problems which can tend to outweigh its advantages. Composed entirely of lines, these drawings tend to be light in contrast, making them generally a poor choice for group presentations, as they cannot be seen clearly from a distance. This low contrast can even make it difficult for designers to achieve a precise picture of the drawing in progress.

When completed, the tonal value of the solids remains the same as the spaces they form, which can diminish the importance of the relationship between the two. Similarly, designers who use a single line to delineate spaces within a plan may not convey, either to themselves or an intended audience, the actual impact of the spaces that are being created. Changing the hierarchy between solid and void by poché, hatching, or perhaps a simple thickening of the lines may help to minimize the abstraction caused by inadequate line application.

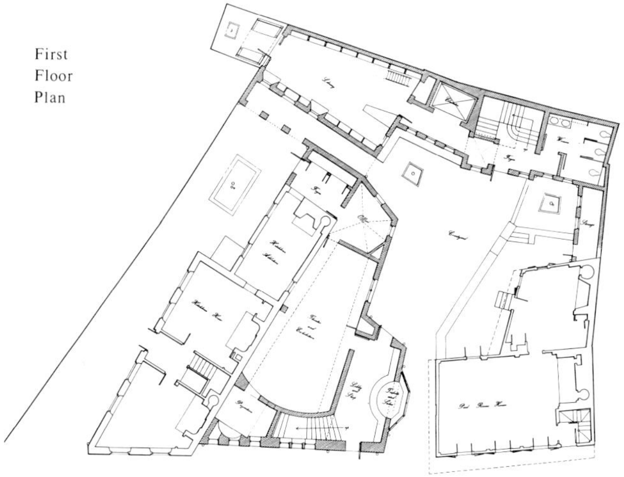

First Floor Plan

Figure 1.15
The plans for a historical museum are treated with hatched poché, while existing buildings are drawn with simple lines. A light source from the upper right has also been assumed, with heavier line weights being used to depict "shadows."

Poché and Building Plans

The use of poché in building plans is an old and accepted technique in producing drawings of high contrast and bold presentation value. As these plans are usually produced by "filling in" the constructed solids of a line drawing, they are more time-consuming and, once completed, are more difficult to change. Some designers, however, have learned to use a thick pen, marker, or pencil to produce bold, poched walls with a single stroke. If handled skillfully, good results can be easier to produce than with a double line drawing. The building plan using poché has many of the advantages of the figure ground, primarily the forceful determination of built solid as opposed to unbuilt void. This allows volumes of space to be configured and developed with greater clarity than in a line drawing. A secondary advantage lies in the presentation process, enabling the production of dark and bold drawings which are visible and readable by an audience from a reasonable distance.

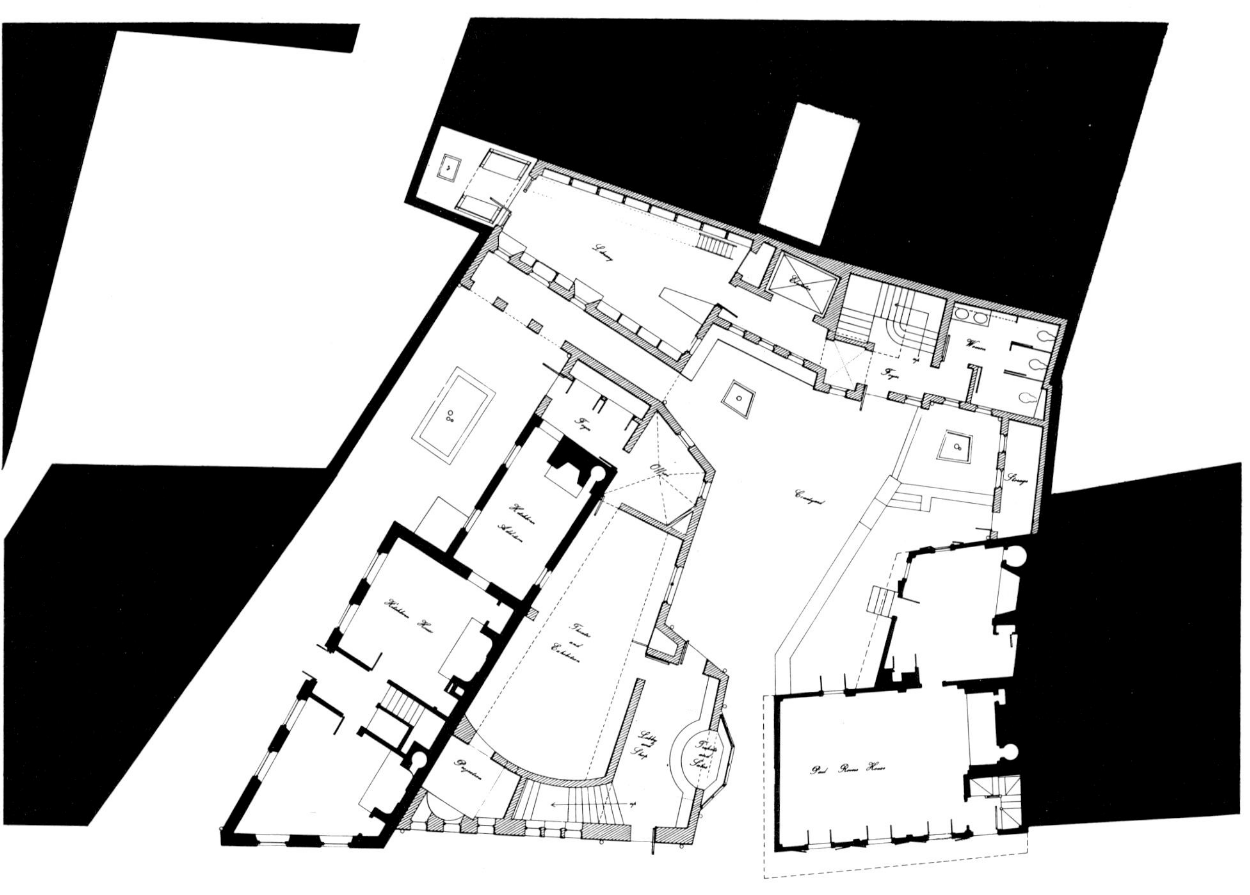

Figure 1.16
Black ink has been used to poché all existing structures, which helps to illustrate how the museum addition has been designed within its context.

Plan Shadowing

Plan shadowing is a technique in which a consistent light source is assumed, and shadows (or their graphic implications) are drawn to produce a three-dimensional inference through the use of depth clues. It is very useful to use in conjunction with plans to depict not only a flat graphic pattern, but enclosed volumes of space. Often a completed line drawing is used, supplemented by a thicker line weight to consistently show the "shaded side" of any built solid. The result is a drawing which resembles a bas-relief model, with walls rising in front of the picture plane, and floor planes receding behind. Stairs, ramps, or areas open to below can be effectively shown by increasing the depth of shadows as they would actually appear. Some drawings may be taken beyond simple line weights, and poché or hatch added to the shadows, although these obviously take more time to complete. They can also create a disturbing figure ground effect, where the shadows become dark "figures" which may make the drawing difficult to read. In some cases, only important spaces should be given shadows, while minor rooms are left as simple line drawings. In many ways, this technique resembles mosaique or reverse figure ground, as it is the ground plane which receives tone, allowing white built solids to rise up from the surface of the drawing.

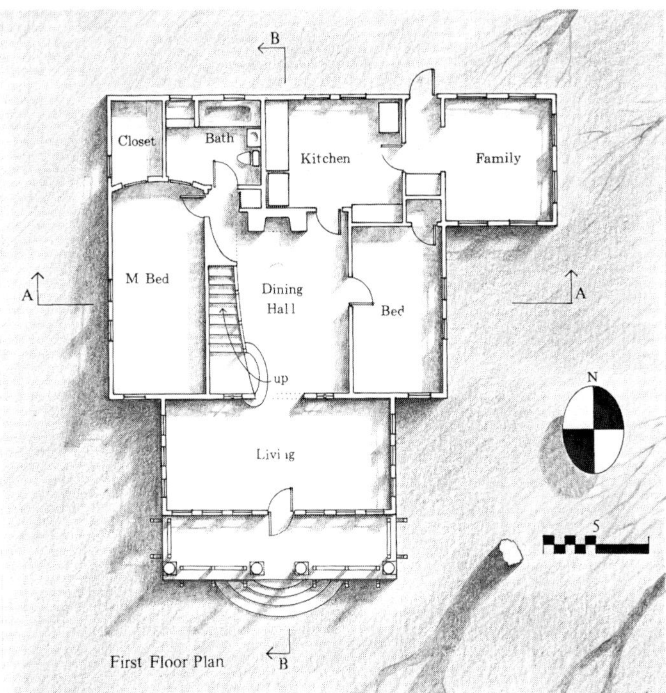

Figure 1.17
Black colored pencil was used to produce this shadowed plan of a summer home. The shadows allow rooms to read as volumes which recede from the picture plane. By varying the length of the cast shadows, even the slope of the site can be described as well as the height of nearby trees.

REFLECTED CEILING PLANS

A reflected ceiling plan is a drawing type which records all information concerning a building's ceiling as if seen in a continuously mirrored floor. Any patterns, textures, or materials can be drawn and studied in direct conjunction with the development of the plan, which enables the latter to describe volumes of space rather than simply flat planes. Although not a technique which is widely used in the design of modern buildings, the reflected ceiling plan (in conjunction with the plan and section) is an excellent tool which can be used to shape and form rooms and provide an internal consistency between all of their surfaces. Typically, dotted lines are used to represent elements above the picture plane, although lightly drawn lines can also be used. At one time, in fact, it was an accepted convention for the shapes of the ceiling plane to be mirrored as literal floor pavement. Tile, brick, and stone joints would describe the vaults, domes, coffers, and beams overhead, helping the plan to become a truly spatial design device.

Figure 1.18
This temple plan demonstrates the idea of a reflected ceiling plan, drawn as if the floor were covered by mirrors and accurately reflecting every beam, coffer, and ornamental molding.

PLAN PERSPECTIVES

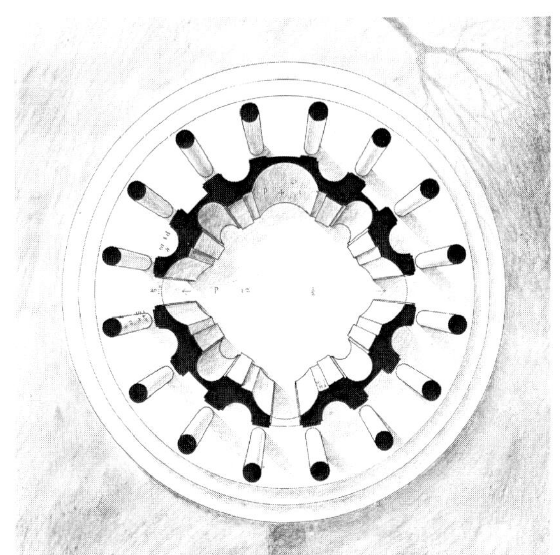

Figure 1.19
A plan perspective of a small round temple was drawn in ink and then shadowed with black colored pencil.

Composite plan types are plans which are combined with other drawing conventions to provide multiple combinations of information. The plan-perspective is a good example of this technique. Usually, the plan is used as a base drawing from which a one-point bird's-eye perspective is constructed, placing the vanishing point in the space of most importance. These drawings are very useful for purposes of presentation, allowing rooms to be viewed as literal volumes while enabling all their wall surfaces to be seen in conjunction with the plan. Although they sound complicated, plan perspectives are useful in presenting ideas to a lay audience, where the composite arrangement of information can be more comprehensible than in traditional drawing types.

Variations in the plan perspective include varying the eye level, causing a slightly elevated viewpoint as if the building were under construction. Frank Lloyd Wright made use of this technique while designing, although the severe distortion and construction difficulties which can arise in their drafting tends to limit their use in the design process.

PLAN OBLIQUES

Pre-nineteenth-century cartographers and architectural engravers developed the interesting convention of adding to site plans certain elements drawn in oblique (paraline). While a principal building may be drawn in true plan, entourage (trees, hedges, other landscape elements) could be drawn in oblique view, seeming almost to "stand up" from the plan in the third dimension. Conversely in some site plans, major buildings can be found drawn in oblique, while minor elements remain in true plan. The results achieved with this technique seem sometimes "naive" in character, resembling the true-plan, true-elevation nature of medieval depiction. However, this remains a technique not to be overlooked. It allows designers to quickly transform flat site plans into communicative, spatial drawings, or helps the viewer focus upon the more important information drawn in oblique.

Plan obliques are also useful in showing rooms as volumes of space, and they are easier and quicker to prepare than perspectives. A true plan is used, and then rooms are "dropped down." Doors, windows, and other vertical elements can then be drawn and developed in conjunction with the plan.

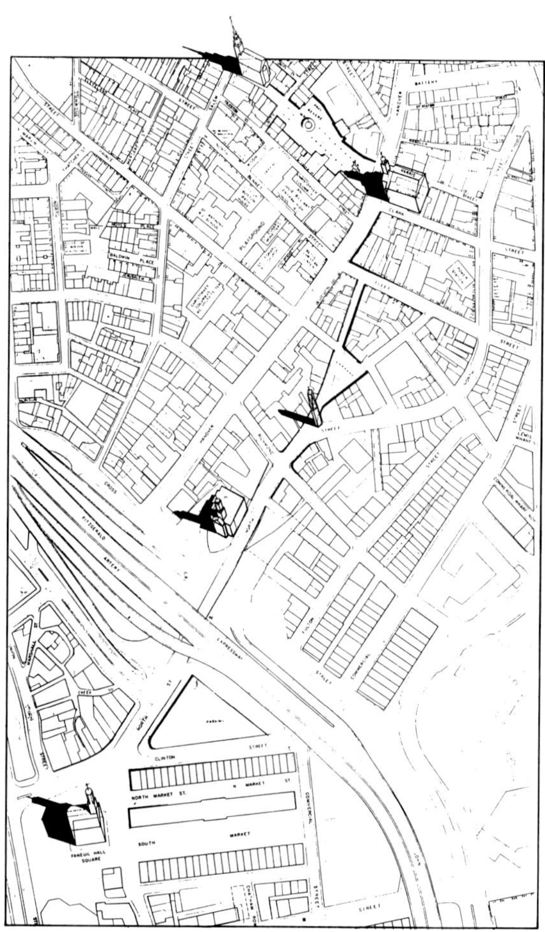

Figure 1.20
Boston's old North End, drawn in plan oblique. The drawing depicts only towers and cupolas in oblique, while the rest of the urban fabric remains in flat plan. Black shadows were cast to emphasize the height of the towers and the path connecting them.

EXPLODED PLANS

Exploded plans show the individual floors of a building in a single graphic image. Typically, they are drawn as if the various levels of a building were hovering one above the other, while dotted lines are used to connect the corners and clarify their interrelationships. One advantage of this type of drawing is that the entire organization of a building can be seen at once, which can encourage a designer to develop unity and connections between different floor levels.

Figure 1.21
An exploded plan of a resort hotel shows how the typical upper levels relate to the complex ground floor services in a single drawing. Dotted lines connect critical corners and help to provide depth clues by means of overlap.

BUILDING DESIGN AND THE SECTION

As previously described, it is possible to take a single plan and develop it for several completely different sections, with volumes and surfaces so different as to make them seem unrelated. By contrast, two well-coordinated sections can only have one corresponding plan. The point here is to underscore the primary importance of the sectional view, since in this drawing the shapes and surfaces of spaces can be determined with closer correspondence to the built world than is possible in the plan. Many experienced designers begin not in plan, but in section. For example, Louis Kahn's early design sketches for the Kimball Art Museum principally involved sectional sketches through the vaults, enabling the full development of their shape, construction, and lighting from which the plan configuration could then grow. It is interesting to note that inexperienced designers often tend to regard the section as the least important drawing, which may only be started after the plans and elevations have been finalized.

The variety of sectional drawing types tends to be closely related to planometric alternatives. If plans are conceived as horizontal sections, sections are vertical plans, so that many of the techniques discussed in plan types are directly applicable to sectional drawings.

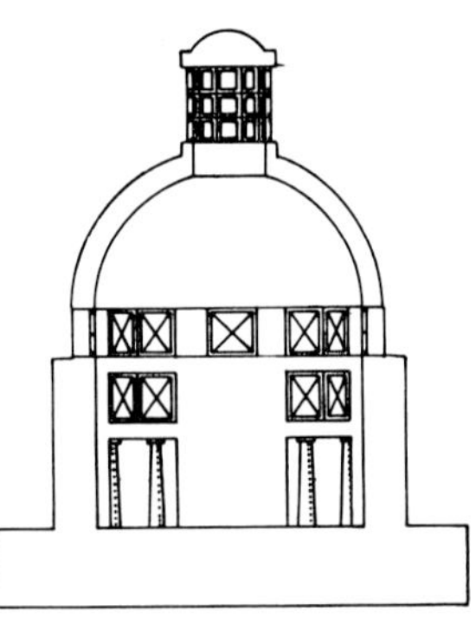

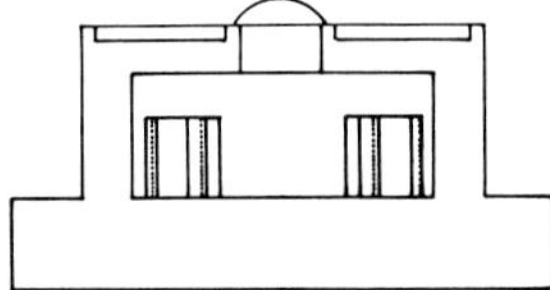

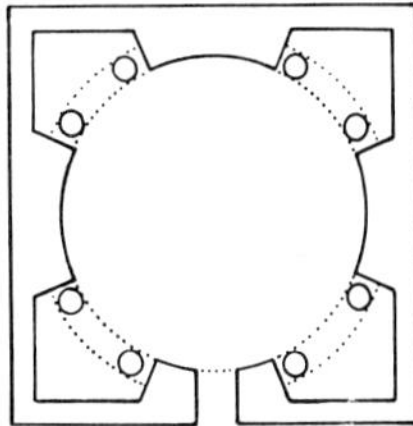

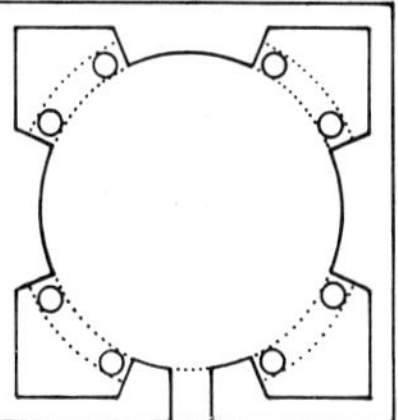

Figure 1.22
Completely different sections, developed for a single plan, demonstrate the significance of the section in architectural design.

LINE DRAWINGS

The most typically drawn section is the line drawing which, while fast to execute and easy to modify, is not the most powerful presentation drawing. It tends to use the same convention (i.e., of undifferentiated white space) for both built solid and unbuilt void, creating a poor figure ground contrast. Of course, certain graphic techniques can help to address this problem. Elements cut in section can be drawn with a heavy line weight, while elements seen in elevation beyond are drawn much lighter. If properly handled, this system can greatly reduce the problems of figure ground and can bring depth clues into an otherwise flat drawing. It is also possible here to use a very fine line weight to indicate basic construction details and material uses within wall and floor thicknesses. This can provide valuable information as well as helping the drawing to read more effectively. Alternatively, sectional line drawings are often constructed with the intention of adding color or poché at a later stage.

Line drawings of individual rooms or volumes are sometimes drawn as figures isolated from the building which contains them. Once the limits and basic configuration of a room have been determined, these drawings can help a designer to think of a room as a discrete entity and not as a void left over after walls and floors have been designed. These drawings can be useful for the study of spaces, such as courtyards or atria. However, although the simplification and abstraction of design problems in this way can be useful, working on a space in complete isolation from its context can be detrimental to the overall design. It should therefore be used for greatest effect in conjunction with other, more comprehensive drawing types.

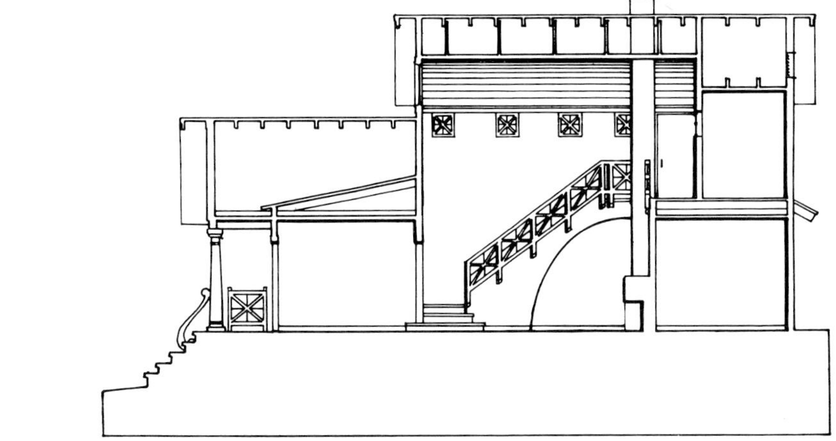

Figure 1.23
The illustration shows a building section of a small summer home with the interior elevation of the stair hall. A light source from the upper right has been assumed, and dark lines are used to describe the shadowed surfaces. The section has a large base, the white space of which moves directly up into the wall and stair sections.

POCHÉ AND THE SECTION

Sections with poché have the primary advantage of showing the resolution of built solid and unbuilt void with visual force and clarity. Their employment in the design process can help designers to shape, mold, and texture built solids to form volumes of space. As these drawings are usually executed by filling in a finished line drawing, they tend to take more time to complete. However, it is possible to make use of the pochéd section in initial design sketches by using a thick pencil or pen to quickly draw in the figure ground and shape of the formed rooms.

The sharp contrast which makes poché drawings easier to read than line drawings makes them ideal for presentation purposes, although with solid black poché, it is impossible to add construction details to the built solids. However, if the poché is lightly colored or hatched, further detail can be added.

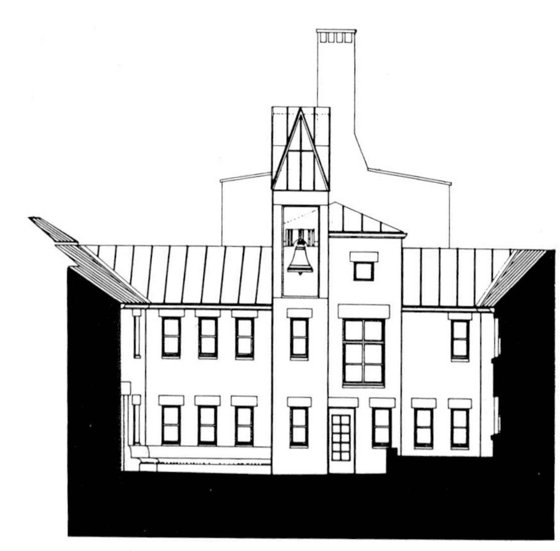

Figure 1.24
The heavy black poché which describes the surrounding buildings frames this courtyard elevation and helps to communicate the designer's concept of discrete, enclosed outdoor rooms.

Figure 1.25
The shape, character, and natural lighting of rooms are emphasized by the black poché of the section cuts. The dark base helps to establish the picture plane from which the rooms recede.

SECTION SHADOWING

Section shadowing is a technique in which a consistent light source is assumed, and the resultant shadows are cast and rendered to make spaces recede (and built solids advance) from the picture plane. This kind of drawing is useful not only in the section, but in the depiction of the interior elevations beyond. These elevations are drawn in a lighter line weight than the section cut, so that shadows can be cast on their features to produce a convincing effect of depth in the drawing. Often a line drawing is used, where a single heavy line is added to consistently show the "shaded side" of any object. If more contrast and depth effect is desired, shadows can be accurately cast and pochéd. If the interior elevations are heavily rendered and shadowed, the built solids should then remain white, resembling the techniques used in reverse figure ground.

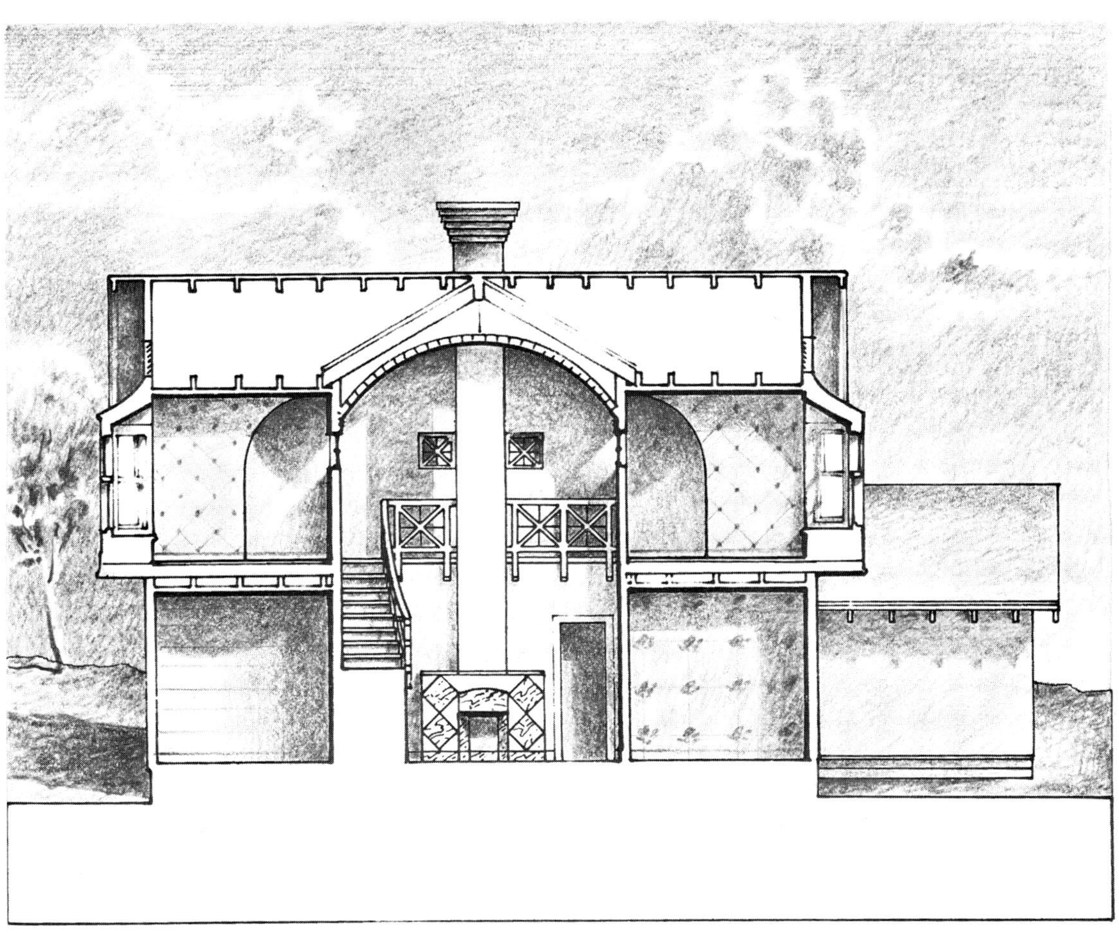

Figure 1.26
Black colored-pencil sciography allows rooms to recede from the picture plane in this shadowed section. The overall background tone of sky, earth, and wall surfaces is essential to a three-dimensional reading of the drawing.

BENT AXIS SECTIONS

Bent axis sections, sometimes referred to as bent picture plane drawings, are used infrequently in current practice, but at one time they were widely accepted as a useful drawing convention. They were primarily used in cross-axis schemes, where the section (with corresponding interior elevations) would first cut down the major axis, then turn at 90 degrees to depict the minor axis. Their use was limited principally to designs with near-absolute axial symmetry, where a straight section would reveal mirror-image redundancy. However, the technique has broader application today, most notably in schemes with curved spaces, axial shifts, or skewed grids, where the section cut can curve, shift, or skew to present all elements of a design both orthogonally and to scale. Although some designers may view this as a technique of distortion providing an unrealistic image, it does allow a section to be shown which reveals more information about a scheme than traditional sections.

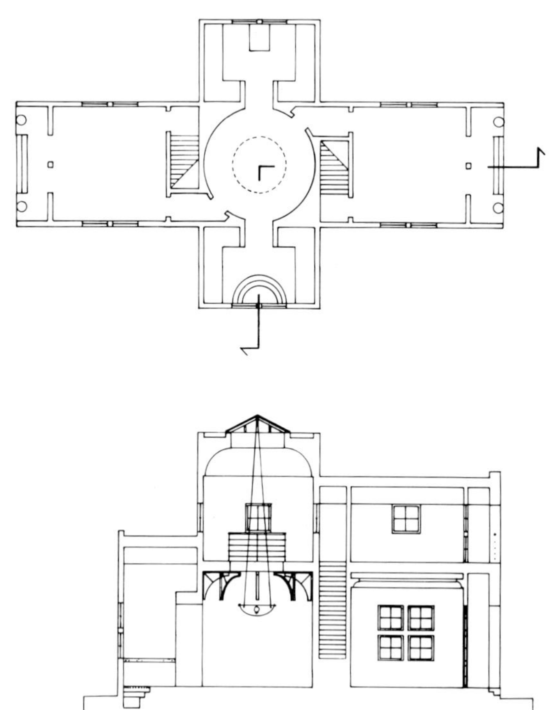

Figure 1.27
A bent axis section of a residential project. The design features near-perfect symmetry about both transverse and longitudinal axes, enabling the use of this drawing technique.

SECTION ELEVATIONS

Figure 1.28
A small chapel drawn as a section elevation in which the two views have been joined as a single image, allowing the designer to make direct observations regarding their interrelationship.

There exists a composite drawing type which was traditionally used to develop and demonstrate the relationship between a building's principal elevation and its major interior space. By drawing both elevation and section as a single image (the two images meeting about the central axis), direct comparisons can be made between the two joined images. While this sort of drawing has long been out of common use, it has a unique characteristic which should not be overlooked. It can compel the designer to develop interior volumes and exterior surfaces simultaneously, designing the two together as a single, unified composition. One can easily understand how a major interior volume expresses itself on a building's primary elevation, and designing with such a drawing type can produce schemes which are better resolved in this respect than those developed with more typical "separate" drawings. The usefulness of these drawings is generally limited to those designs composed with complete bilateral symmetry, and the designer must realize that the drawing type itself may force symmetry upon a scheme. Like many analytical methods, this one presents information in an extremely abstract way, emphasizing some information at the expense of others (i.e., what does the entire elevation really look like?). In addition, it emphasizes certain design ideologies (bilateral symmetry, exterior expression of major interiors, unity between parts, etc.) which may or may not coincide with the design problems at hand, or with the designer's intentions.

SECTION PERSPECTIVES

Composite section drawings combine the features of the section with those of other drawings, the most widely used being the section perspective. To produce an effect of convincing depth while retaining the benefits of the true scale section, one-point perspectives can be constructed which use a section cut for a picture plane. Typically, the major space of the building is depicted, with the vanishing point placed within it at eye level. If it is necessary to show more than one major space in a single drawing, multiple vanishing points can be used, although strange distortions can result from the construction of such drawings.

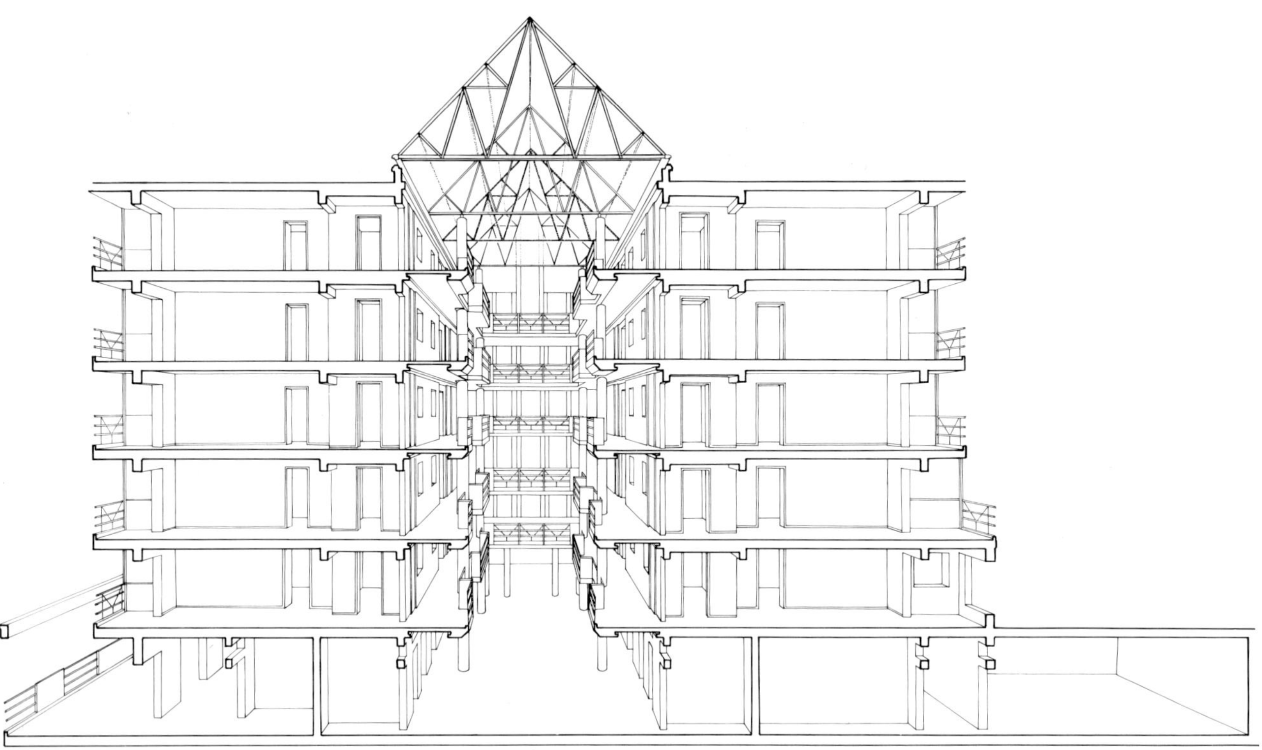

Figure 1.29
Section perspective view of a North Chicago music school project. The heavy line weight which defines the section cut helps in the spatial reading of the drawing.

SECTIONAL OBLIQUES

Sectional obliques are similar to section perspectives, although they are easier to execute. However, as their point of view is usually taken from far above eye level, ceilings and upper wall parts are often shielded from sight. Nevertheless, all elements can be drawn to scale, which makes these drawings useful for design purposes.

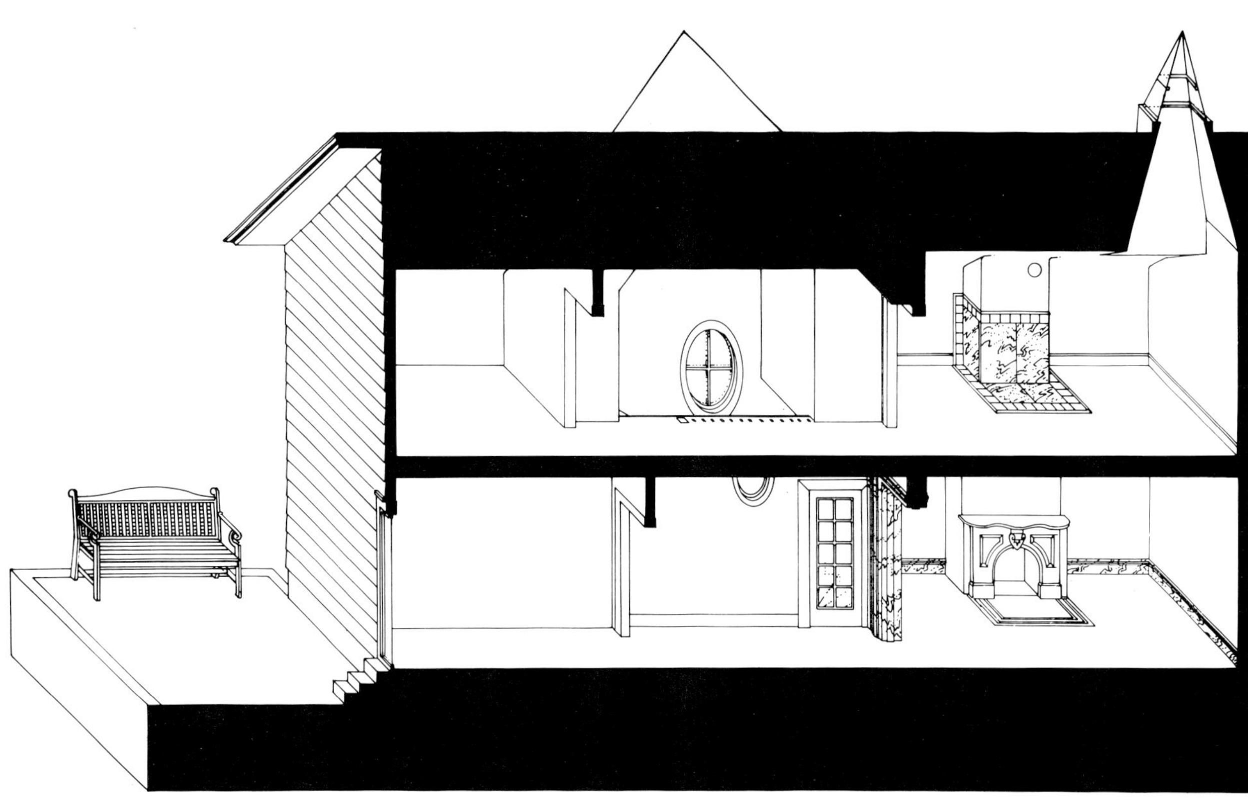

Figure 1.30
The proposed renovation of a Victorian cottage, drawn in the form of a sectional oblique, with black poché used to describe the cut areas. Ease of construction and true scale measurements make this kind of drawing easier to use as a design tool than the section perspective.

ELEVATIONS AND BUILDING DESIGN

The elevation is probably used more often than any other drawing type to determine the exterior appearance of buildings. It can be swiftly generated from plans and sections, and design drawings can be completed in a fraction of the time that it would take to complete perspectives, models, or axonometrics. Like the plan, however, the elevation achieves its speed and simplicity through abstraction, and it has inherent limitations and perceptual distortions. In the real world, we seldom see buildings in true elevation, and only flat, planar surfaces, viewed directly from great distances, resemble elevational images. More typically, we experience buildings while moving through space, seeing them obliquely, foreshortened, and in perspective. To design a building from a viewpoint that may never be perceived is hardly the ideal approach. For example, roofs which may appear as powerful elements in elevation may recede in importance and even be unnoticeable in the completed building when viewed from the ground level. Such distortions occur frequently. The limitations of the pure elevation, then, must be kept in mind while designing.

The difficulties of describing three-dimensional objects with pure elevations can have other negative effects on the design process. As the elevation is an inherently flat and dimensionless medium, it tends to encourage the design of flat building surfaces. It does not lend itself to the investigation of the three-dimensional properties of the design, or, if constructed as a simple line drawing, indicate the potential effects of light and shade on the created forms. However, there are several types of elevation drawings which, if used in appropriate design and presentation situations, can help to overcome these problems. These are outlined in the remainder of the chapter.

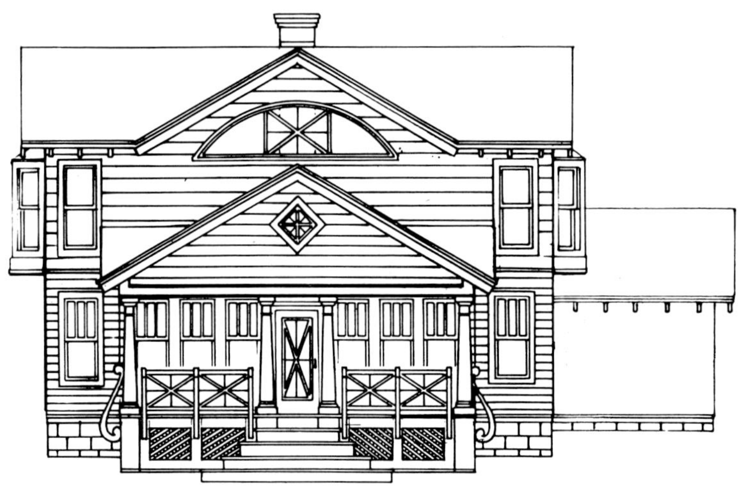

Figure 1.31
Elevation of a lakeside summer home. Depth clues are primarily provided by overlap, with some line weight variation.

LINE AND THE ELEVATION

The kind of elevation most typically produced is the line drawing. Used primarily for simplicity and speed of execution, these drawings often sacrifice information. For example, a brick wall, a sheet of glass, and the sky beyond can all be represented by undifferentiated white space, while the joints between these surfaces may all be represented by a single line. To expect such a drawing to accurately depict what the building will look like is unrealistic. However, the ability of the line drawing to enable the designer to study shape, size, and proportion in quick reiterations does make it a useful tool.

The key to making line drawings readable is primarily in the choice of line weight. A typical method used to choose line weights is the imitation of atmospheric perspective by drawing near objects in heavy lines and distant objects in light ones, with a gradated range in between. This can help to simulate the recession of planes or objects in space. Another technique utilizes heavy lines at major building edges (corners, returns, etc.) and handles all detail and fenestration on a plane in light lines, regardless of their nearness. This can be used to clarify a building's major elements, although drawings of this nature can appear to be spatially flat.

Figure 1.32
Excerpt from a first-place competition design for a dormitory on the University of Wisconsin/Madison campus. The elevation rests on a section cut through the earth which denotes grade changes near the building.

FIGURE GROUND ELEVATIONS

The use of the figure ground in elevation is unusual, but it can be useful in studying the pattern of fenestration on a facade. By using poché to blacken windows, a designer can judge more clearly the size, position, proportion, and rhythm of openings in a design than with a line drawing. The technique is obviously best suited to the study of designs with more traditional wall-window relationships than, for example, a glass curtain wall. Although the use of this drawing type may produce extremely high contrast drawings that seem abstract in a graphic sense, windows in most wall surfaces appear in high contrast when seen in reality. The figure ground elevation can therefore be an appropriate analytical drawing type.

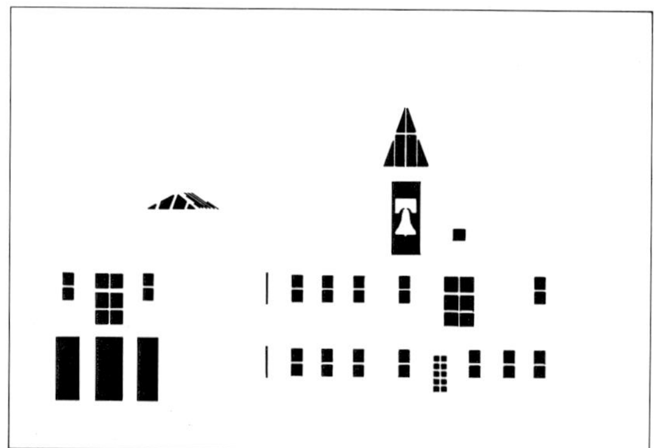

Figure 1.33
Top: Site section with courtyard elevations drawn with linework only. A light source from the upper right has been assumed, and heavy lines have been used to denote window depth.
Middle: A figure ground elevation, in which all window openings receive black poché. The pattern, rhythm, and size of openings are much more apparent than in the line drawing.
Bottom: Reverse figure ground elevation, which resembles a night view of the courtyards.

ELEVATION SHADOWING

Elevation shadowing is a technique in which a constant light source is assumed, and shadows are cast to depict objects as they might actually appear. The length of shadows and their accurate configurations can then actually be constructed and rendered. Often, shadows on wall surfaces are cast in hatching or grey tone, while shadows on windows are black or very dark. Accurate shadow casting can allow a flat elevation to convincingly communicate the depth of recession and projection on a flat plane. Of course, the construction and rendering of accurate shadows is difficult and time consuming, and simpler techniques are often used. For example, a single heavy line can be drawn to indicate the shadow cast by an object, while edges upon which light is falling are sometimes not drawn at all. In drawing a window, therefore, the shadowed head and one jamb may be drawn, but the opposite jamb and the sill omitted. This system is best used on small drawings in which the illustration of detail is difficult. Surface textures, such as stone joints or window mullions, can also be drawn in this way.

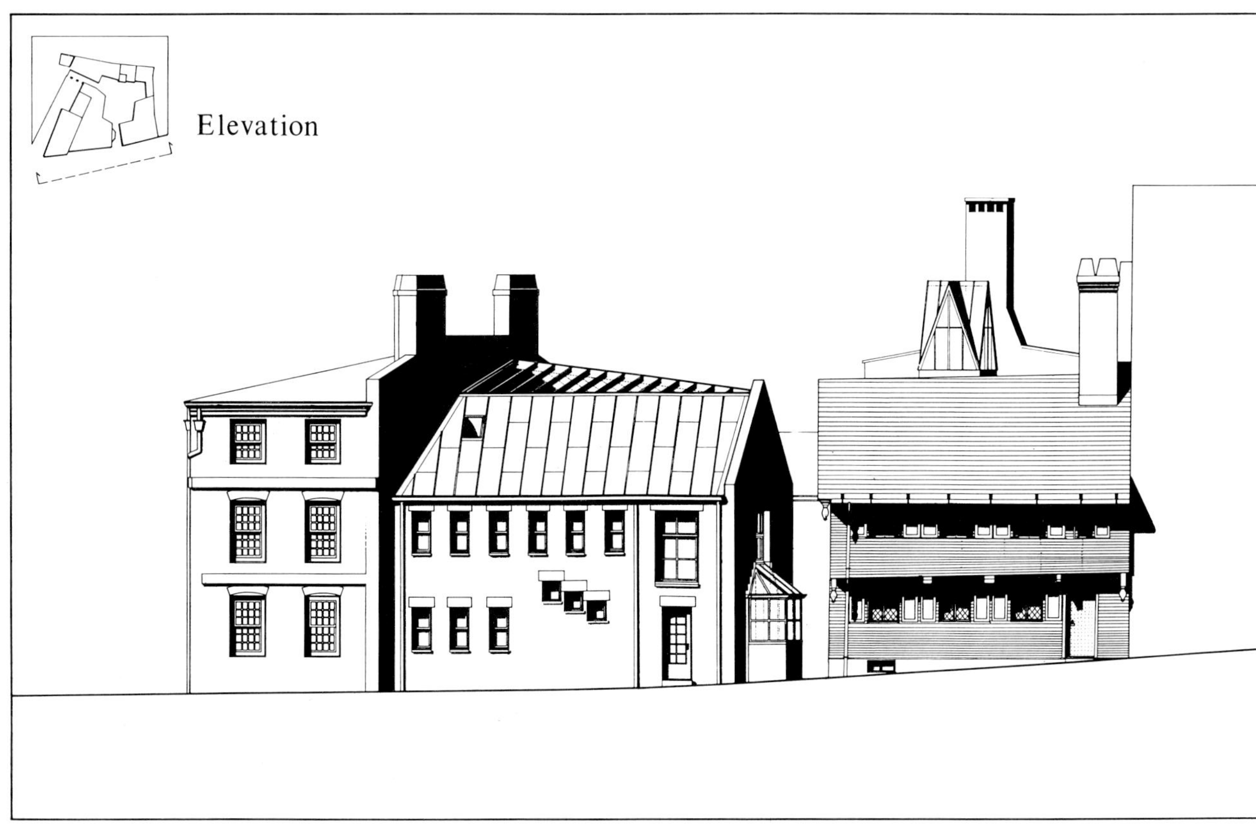

Figure 1.34
Shadowed contextural elevation of a small museum building. Afternoon sun is assumed, with all surfaces in shadow receiving black poché. The shadows accurately denote window and overhang depths. Drawings which utilize black shadows can sometimes assume a harsh, almost sinister appearance, and they may not be appropriate to some schemes.

“SKEWED” ELEVATIONS

“Skewed” elevations can be produced when a picture plane is placed askew to an orthogonal building. They may be useful in contexts where nearby buildings sit with different orientations, and where a contextual elevation can show some structures “corner on.” A building drawn in such a way has the disadvantage of not being to scale, as all horizontal dimensions appear foreshortened. However, these drawings are sometimes more descriptive of form than regular elevations, showing two elevations simultaneously. They may therefore be used if a building is intended to be seen obliquely, as in the case of a street corner scheme.

The skewed elevation has limited application in the design process but can be used to dramatic effect in presentations.

Figure 1.35
The skewed elevation technique was used in this freehand sketch of an urban garden at the tip of a triangular city block. The “skewed” surfaces are shadowed to reveal mass and help provide depth clues.

Figure 1.36
Design sketch depicting a courtyard addition to a Milwaukee residence. The shadows allow the courtyard to be read as an enclosed room, and they illustrate depth of recession for windows and overhangs.

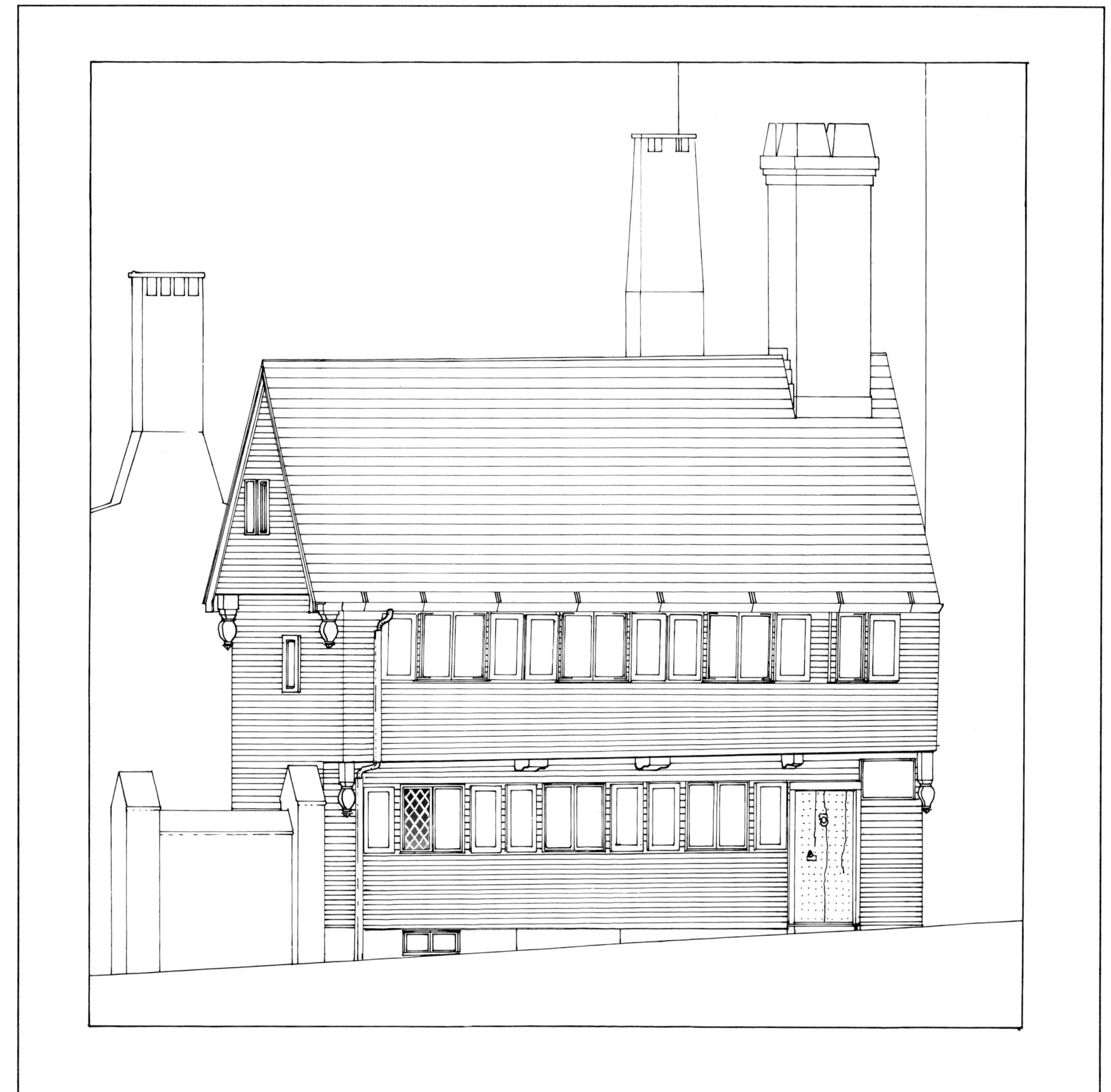

Figure 1.37
Paul Revere's restored home in Boston is drawn in a skewed elevation which emphasizes the three-dimensional form of the building. Usually, these drawings describe mass at the expense of true dimensions, but here the front elevation is drawn to true shape, with only the side (gabled) elevation foreshortened.

UNFOLDED ELEVATIONS

Unfolded, or bent picture plane, elevations can be used when contiguous elevations about a space or a building need to be studied together. All four elevations of a courtyard, for example, can be "unfolded" and drawn together as a single plane. The advantage here is that elevations that will be seen together in a completed building can be drawn and designed to produce a continuous and unified effect, which may be preferable to studying them as separate elements. This notion of "unfolding" is appropriate in a number of situations, such as in the design of atria, squares, or rooms where the elevations should be studied as a single entity. It can also be employed to study curved surfaces by actually curving the picture plane so that all elements appear true to scale and proportional, without the foreshortening effect that elevations of curved surfaces normally provide. Furthermore, unfolded elevations can be combined with a plan of a space, with its corresponding elevations folded down onto a single picture plane. A reflected ceiling plan could be included, too, so that the drawing might even be cut up and folded into a complete model of a room. The ability to see and work to scale on all six surfaces of a room simultaneously has obvious design advantages.

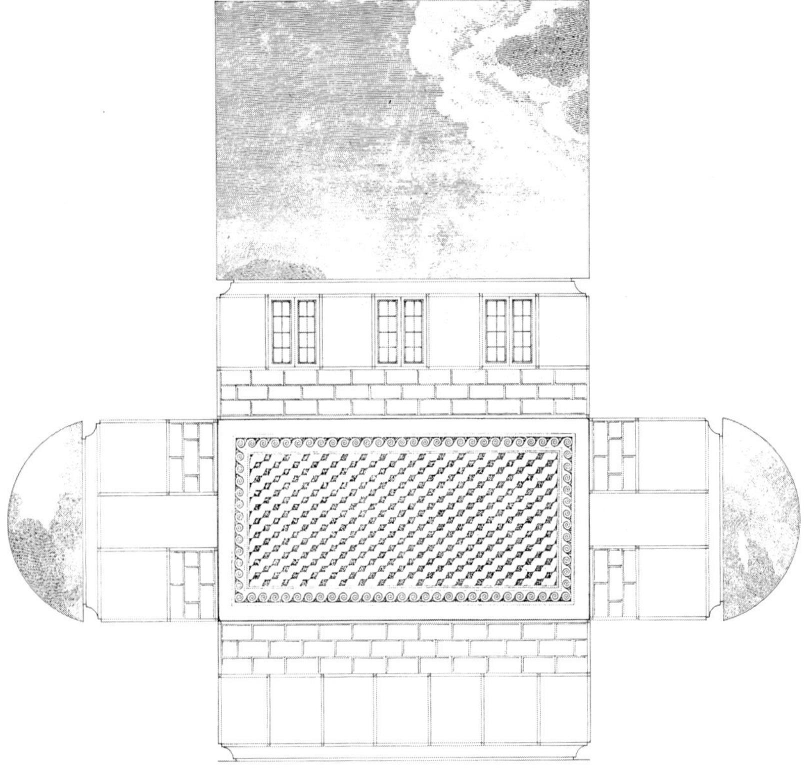

Figure 1.38
All six surfaces of a dining room are unfolded to illustrate every aspect of the design in a single image. Later, the drawing was copied, cut, and folded into a simple model of the room. The scheme featured an elaborate painted floor, faux stonework, and a ceiling vault with a false painted sky.

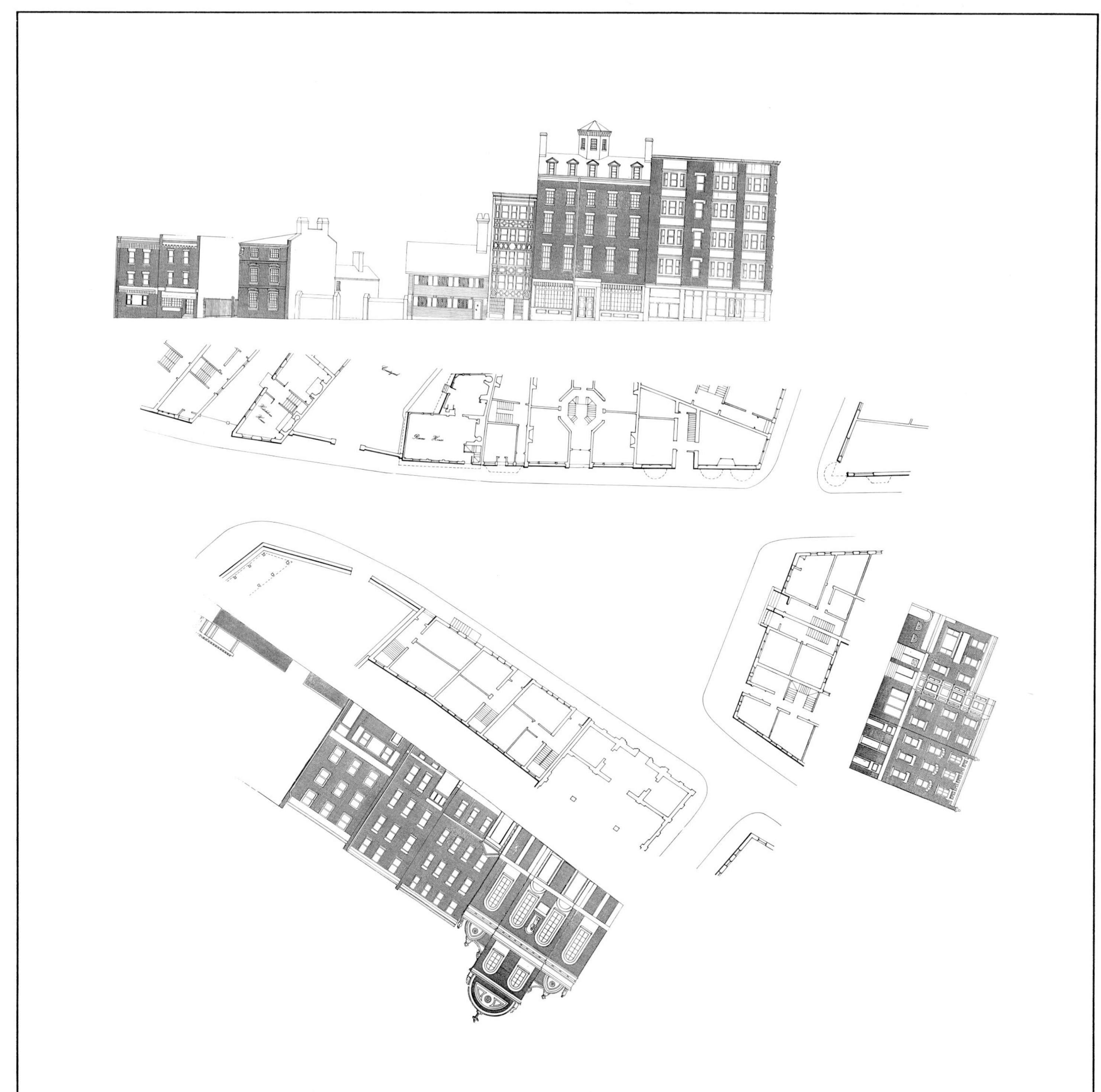

Figure 1.39
The plan and all three elevations of Boston's North Square have been unfolded onto a single plane. The unfolded elevation allows a designer to see and configure all surfaces of a space together in direct relationship to one another.

REGULATING LINES

Regulating lines, or trace regulateurs as they are sometimes called, are light lines overlaying an elevation which serve to demonstrate and clarify the geometric construction or proportional system used in the building's design. The most typical use of regulating lines is probably the description of golden-section proportioning of elevations. The geometric layout of these golden rectangles will actually be drawn (lightly, or in a contrasting color, such as red) directly onto a finished elevation. Often, the diagonal of the rectangle is drawn, as all rectangles which have parallel or perpendicular diagonals are proportionally similar. Sometimes more complicated constructions are recorded on a drawing, such as center points and compass swings. Regulating lines can help to clarify the process and intent of the design, giving finished drawings a sense of design application which is usually seen only in design sketches.

This device is also used occasionally in both plan and section drawings, usually to demonstrate axial layout or an underlying geometric order.

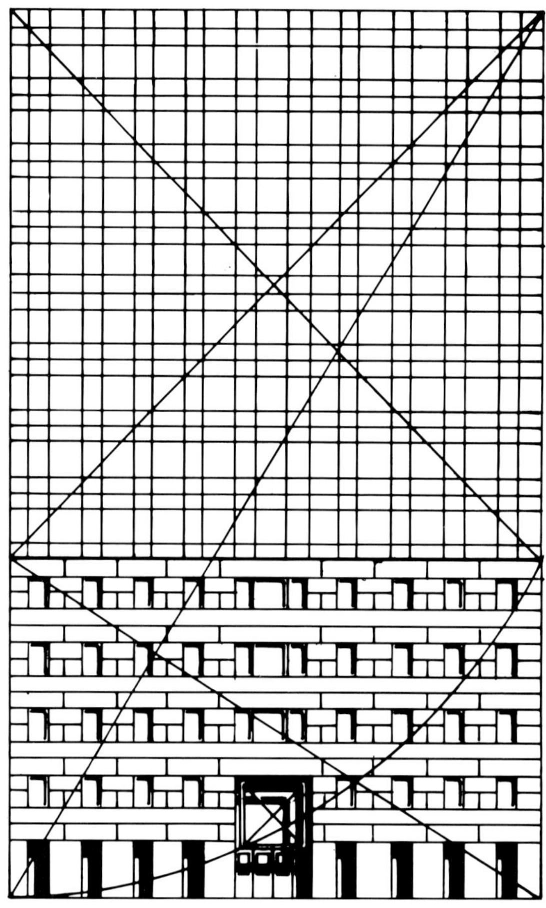

Figure 1.40
This elevation study of a corporate office building makes use of regulating lines to clearly describe the underlying proportional intentions of the scheme. Every element of the stone and glass tower is controlled by golden-section and square relationships.

Chapter Two

Paraline Projection: Axonometric and Oblique Drawings

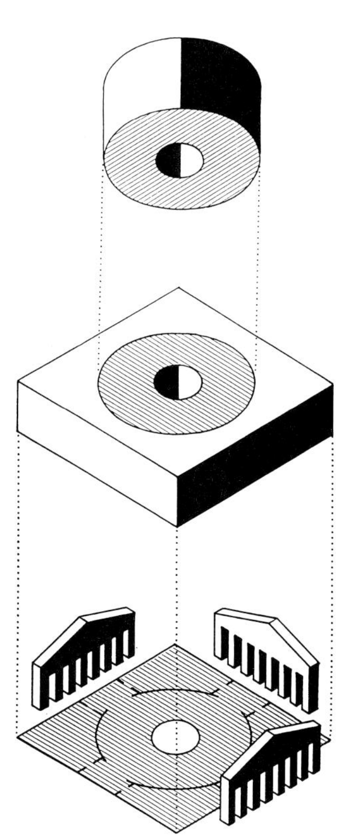

Although axonometric and oblique drawings are by no means recent developments in graphic representation, only in the twentieth century have they become one of the most widely used techniques of design and presentation. Their initial attractiveness to modern architects, it has been suggested, lay not only in their novelty, but in the objective and scientific nature of the images generated, which would have been compatible with the prevailing ideological preferences espoused by the pioneers of the Modern Movement. Drawing on techniques developed from engineering disciplines, architects could use paraline projection to depict a sense of rational detachment which would not be possible with more conventional and subjective techniques.

In addition to any ideological preference, paraline drawings also provide the designer with considerable information in a single drawing. At least two elevations can be shown simultaneously, as well as building massing, plan configuration, and even surrounding site information. The ability to conceive of, and therefore develop and present, multiple aspects of the design in one drawing has made the use of paraline drawings a valuable technique, although certain shortcomings in their use should be recognized to prevent them from being used inappropriately.

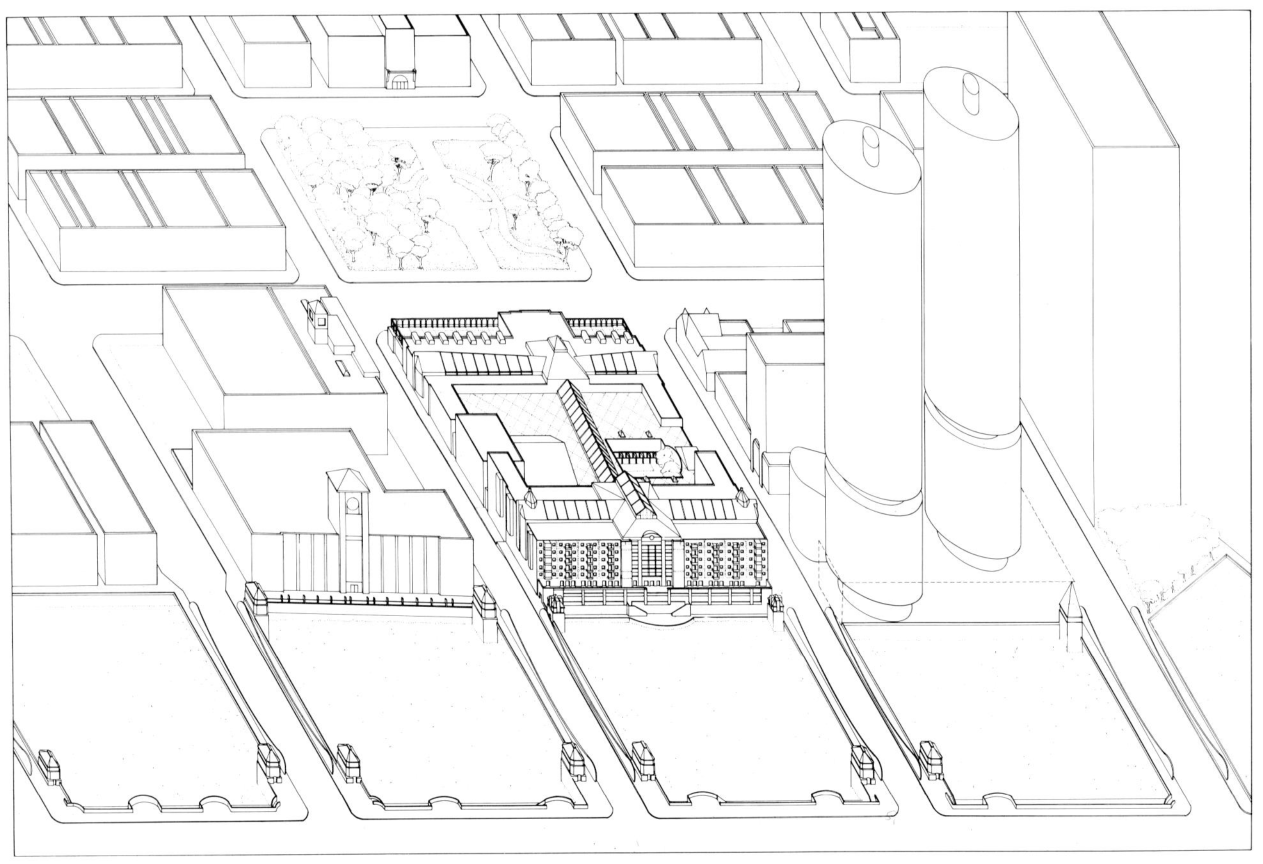

Figure 2.1
A project for a mixed-use development on the Chicago River, near the Marina Towers.

THE ELEVATED VIEWPOINT

The typical axonometric or oblique drawing is constructed with a high viewpoint, as if seen from an airplane. This provides a revealing overview of the subject matter, although from a point of vantage which few observers are likely to occupy when the building is completed. If the drawing is used as a design tool, therefore, there is a danger that the building may be conceived with an unrealistic bias, and that design decisions that are visually important from the ground plane will be inadequately resolved. This problem arises from the nature of the drawing type which, particularly in the case of the oblique, presents the roof plane as the dominant undistorted facade, treating it almost as an elevation. By contrast, the elevations themselves are distorted into acute parallelograms, which tend to make them appear secondary in importance to the roof and may make design decisions involving vertical surfaces more difficult. Facade details and fenestration, for example, can appear overly complex when drawn obliquely, leading to potentially inaccurate decisions by the designer in the size, scale, and proportion of the elevational elements.

Figure 2.2
Oblique view of a scheme for Milwaukee's Watertower Square area. The oblique, drawn here with a true plan, illustrates the extremely high aerial point of view found in many paraline drawings.

OBJECTS IN THE VOID

Paraline drawings are often used in industrial design and engineering, where machine parts and structural connections can be designed and drawn with great clarity and dimensional precision.

Similarly, these drawings can also show individual buildings to great effect, particularly where the form is conceived as a singular, isolated object, as in the case of Le Corbusier's Villa Savoye. However, they are less suitable in the depiction of spaces. An axonometric of a street, for instance, will contain limited information beyond that of the roofscape. One street elevation will be omitted completely, while the other may be obscured by the roofs of the buildings opposite. The ground plane, particularly in narrow streets flanked by high buildings, is unlikely to be seen at all.

It is reasonable to infer, therefore, that the use of paraline drawing tends to favor objects over space, and excessive reliance on the technique may result in less consideration of the spatial aspects of a design. For this reason, it is important to use axonometrics and obliques in conjunction with other drawing types to ensure that all aspects of a scheme are fully explored.

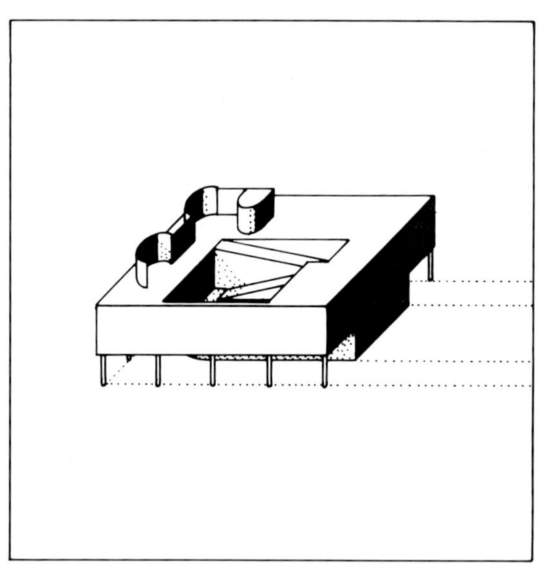

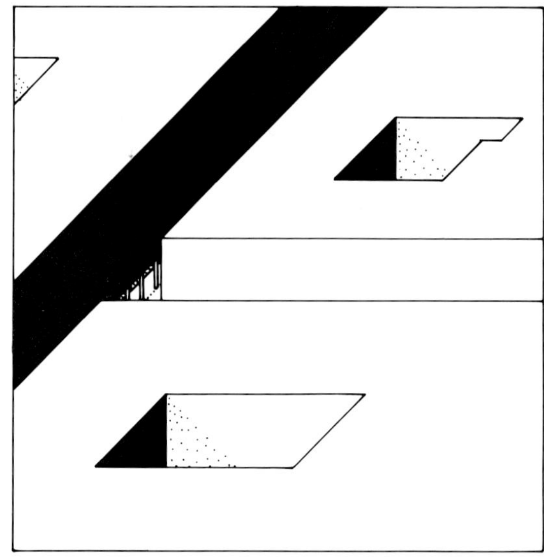

Figure 2.3
Top: An oblique paraline schematic of Le Corbusier's Villa Savoye, demonstrating the ideal nature of paralines in the depiction of free-standing objects in space.
Bottom: This oblique of narrow Parisian streets shows the difficulty of describing enclosed spaces with the paraline view. The drawing reveals only the rooftops, omitting most of the critical information about the character of the spaces below.

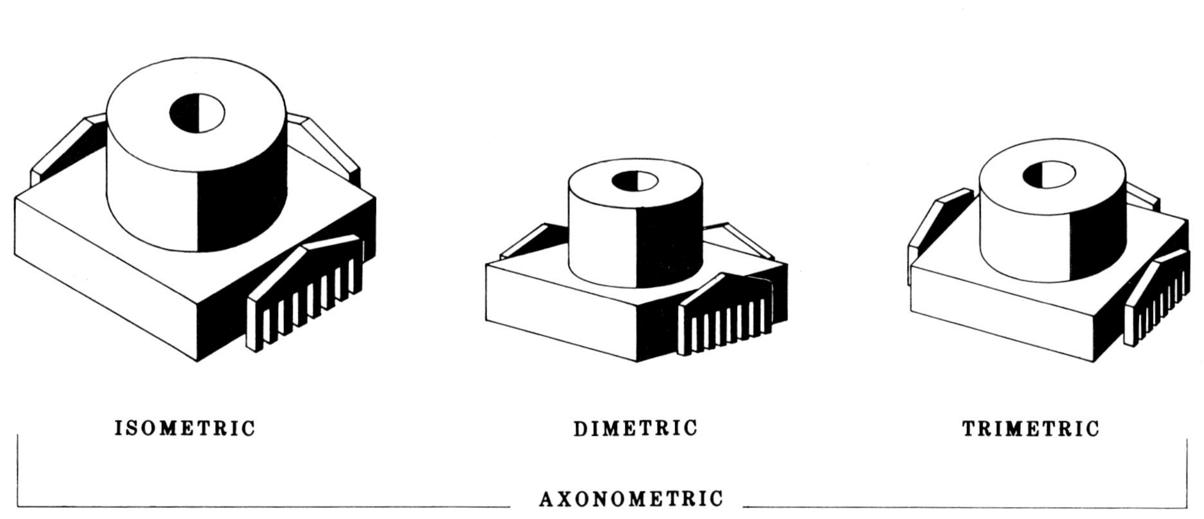

Figure 2.4
A paraline comparison chart, with a schematic view of C. N. Ledoux's Barrier at La Villette drawn in each of the six major paraline types. Note especially the large apparent size of the building when drawn in isometric and cavalier, and the apparent reduction of size and lowering of viewpoint as recession scales are introduced.

Paraline Drawings—Technical Nomenclature

Architects generally refer to any paraline drawing as either an "axonometric" or an "isometric." However, these terms are usually used incorrectly, and a precise system of categories has been developed, primarily for use in technical and industrial illustration. The categories are quite specific, although the nomenclature can seem overly complex. For example, the kind of paraline drawing most typically used by architects and widely called an axonometric would technically be referred to as a "Cavalier—Plan—Oblique." It is perhaps understandable that the system has not caught on with architects. However, as the divisions between paraline types are significant, their applications can influence the design process, so some examination of the alternatives is advisable.

The principal difference between paraline drawing types lies in the level of foreshortening of the receding axes. This foreshortening represents an attempt to bestow upon paraline drawings the pictorial effects seen by the eye in linear perspective, while retaining the advantages of easy construction and scaled measurement. Oddly enough, the techniques which permit a sense of foreshortening and thereby enhance the level of realism in drawings tend to be used more in the field of industrial engineering, while architects appear to favor the simplest and more visually distorted paraline drawing types. However, an examination of the techniques available may help to highlight their potential uses in the design and presentation processes. Paraline drawings are divided into two separate categories: axonometrics and obliques.

Axonometrics

There are three types of axonometric drawings: isometric, dimetric, and trimetric. The word isometric means of "equal measure," as the same unit of measurement is used on all of the drawing's receding axes. As in all axonometrics, the visible surfaces of a rectangular solid are distorted into parallelograms. Dimetric drawings attempt to visually correct the optical enlargement and elongation of isometrics by using a foreshortened scale for the receding axes, while trimetrics are the most difficult to draw, requiring three foreshortened scales in their construction.

When correctly constructed, axonometrics have the ability to achieve more realistic pictorial effects than obliques, primarily by simulating the effects of linear perspective. Axonometrics also have a somewhat lower aerial viewpoint than obliques, which many designers consider to be advantageous. Despite these "realistic" effects, axonometrics (especially foreshortened axonometrics) are considered difficult to utilize during the design process, in part because they lack the "true plane" that makes oblique paralines so simple to construct.

Figure 2.5
An axonometric chart demonstrating the basic ways in which isometric, dimetric, and trimetric drawings can be executed. All images are drawn in isometric.
A. Up-view, or "worm's-eye," axonometric, revealing the mass as seen from below, including the building plan. These views sometimes seem strange and detached because of their "floating" appearance.
B. Cut-away (up-view) axonometric, illustrating the building's cross-section and half of the plan. This technique can be useful with axially symmetrical schemes.
C. The down-view, or "bird's-eye," axonometric is the kind of axonometric most typically utilized in architectural design. Mass is well articulated at the expense of the high point of view and loss of "true" shapes.
D. An exploded (down-view) axonometric. The constituent parts of the building are pulled apart for the sake of diagrammatic clarity. The drawings often achieve an abstract, machine-like quality.
E. Cut-away (down-view) axonometric. The project's section and half the plan and mass are all shown.

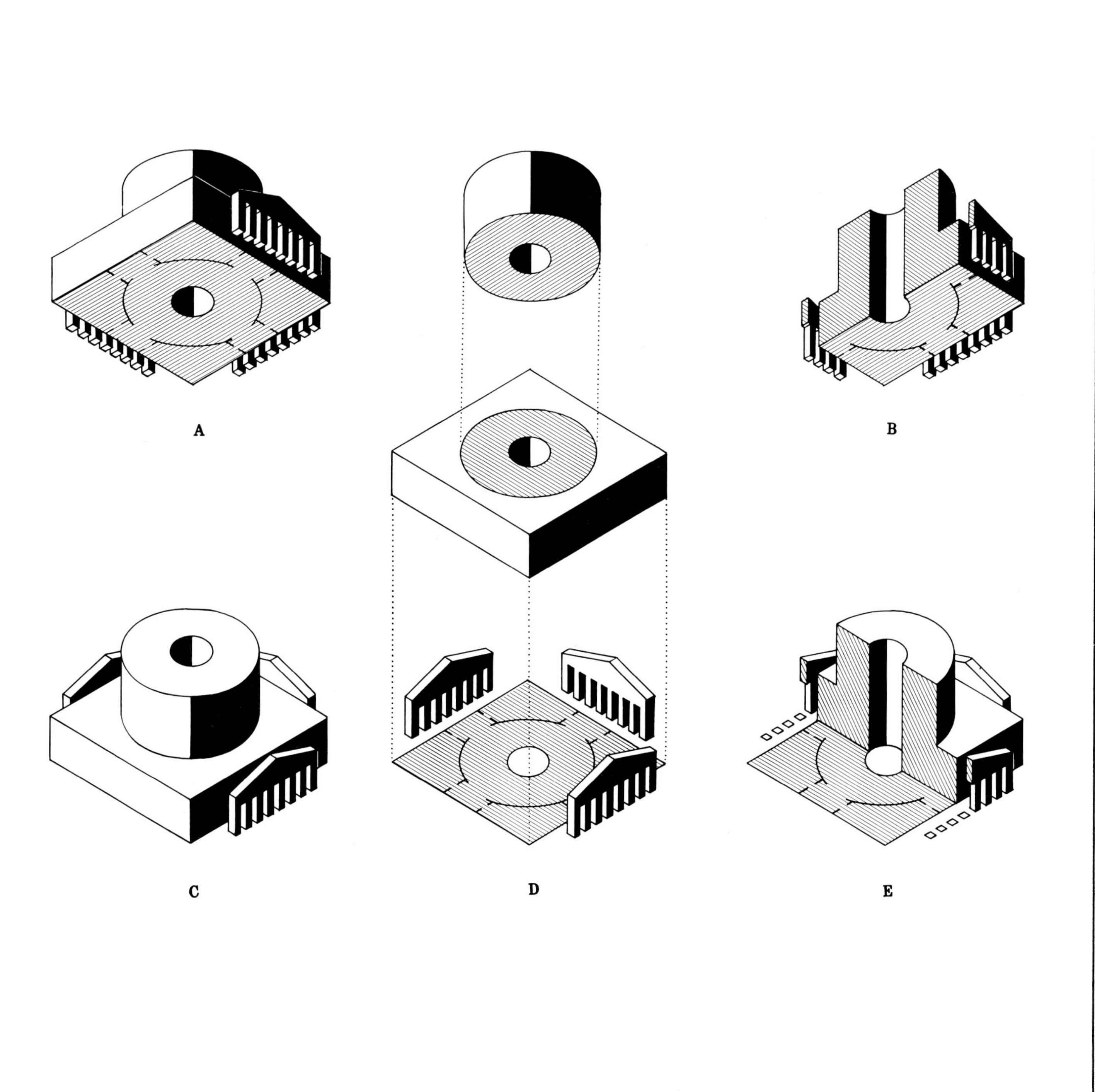

Up-View Axonometrics

Up-view, or "worm's-eye," axonometrics depict a building or space as if viewed from below, looking up through the plan. Perhaps the best-known drawings of this type were published by August Choisy in his *Histoire de L'Architecture* of 1899, in which he presented a wide range of buildings, primarily from the point of view of their construction. The drawing type allowed Choisy to depict, for example, the complete spatial and structural organization of a brick and stone groin vault, recording its plan, sections, elevations, and three-dimensional forms in a single view. The technique represents a curious duality in that while its subterranean point of view is physically impossible, the drawings depict images of facades and rooms in a manner which is closer to real perception of buildings than is normally achieved in other "down-view" paralines. Ceilings, soffits, and wall surfaces usually hidden in typical paralines are all revealed in the up-view. This ability to look up into rooms and at facades from below makes the drawing type unique and makes it a design tool ideally suited for the study of schemes as seen from these points of view (with none of the construction and scale difficulties of perspectives). While it was virtually unknown for many years, this kind of drawing has seen some contemporary resurgence.

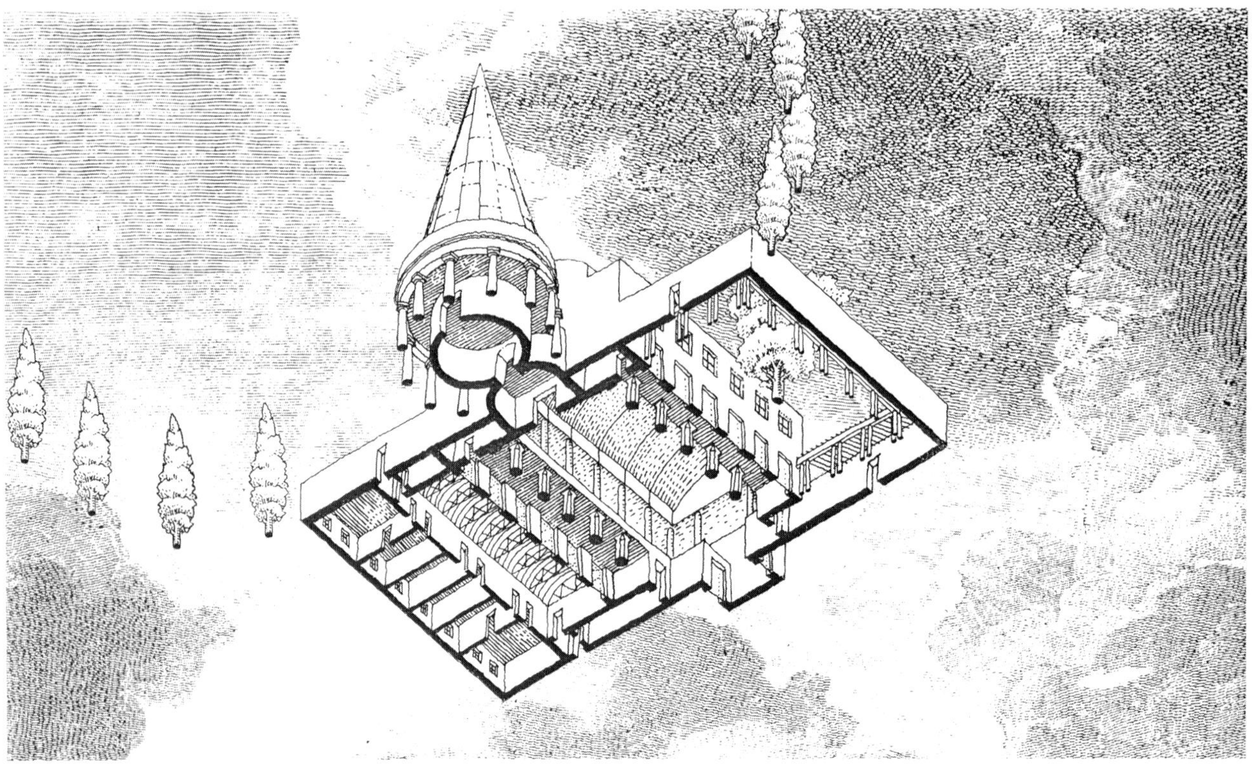

Figure 2.6
This up-view axonometric sketch of a church, cloister, and rectory allows the viewer to look up into rooms and courts and understand the shape and texture of ceilings, soffits, and skylights. The sketch was later cut out and collaged onto an eighteenth-century etching of a sky.

Cut-Away Axonometrics

Both aerial-viewpoint and worm's-eye axonometrics can be drawn as cut-aways, revealing interior spaces which would typically remain hidden. By slicing a design through a primary space or axis and removing foreground axonometric elements, a drawing can be produced which can describe plans, section, and massing in a single view. The principal advantage of this type of drawing is that it can show a major interior volume and describe its relationship to the rest of the composition. This clarity is achieved, however, through the omission of significant portions of a design, which must be removed to reveal the section. This removal of certain elements to reveal the particulars of others is common in paraline drawings, and the decision as to which elements to omit, and how to graphically represent their removal, is a design problem in itself.

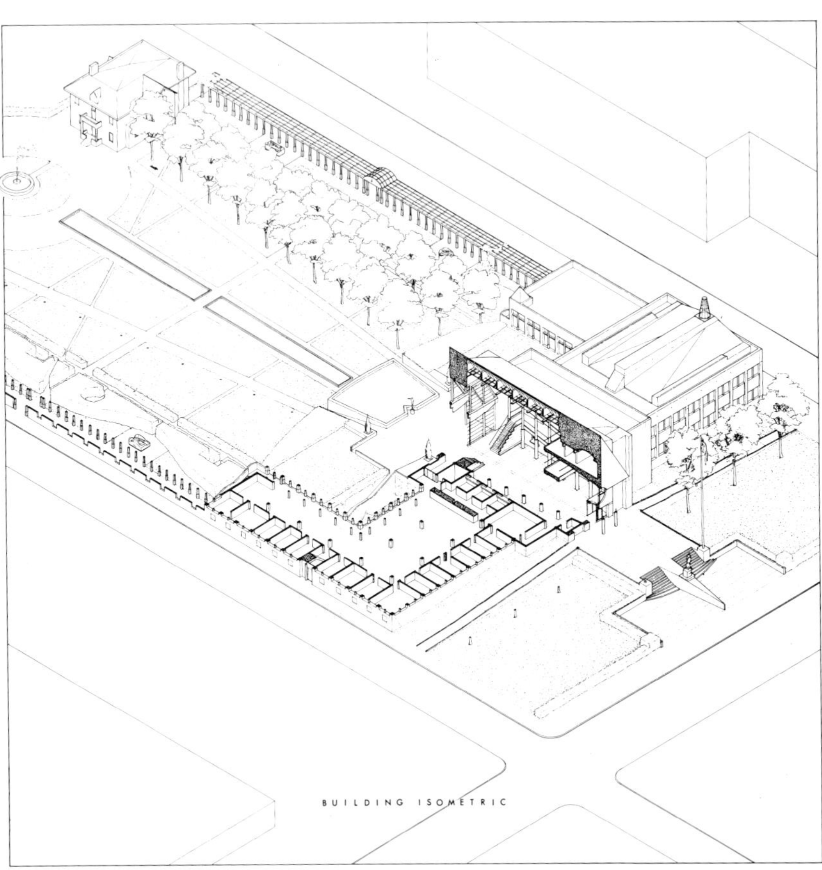

Figure 2.7
Cut-away axonometric of a project for a city hall in Appleton, Wisconsin. The order of the plan, the character of the central hall, and the structure of the gardens are all revealed.

Exploded Axonometrics

Like exploded plans, elements of a complex axonometric drawing can be pulled apart and presented as an "exploded" image. These drawings have a diagrammatic quality and can give the impression of an abstract, analytical tool. Perhaps for this reason they are often used for machine-tool drawings, showing how various elements are assembled. Exploded axonometrics can be useful in architectural drawings, especially in situations where complex construction assemblies must be communicated, and where significant elements of a design which would be hidden in a typical axonometric can be "exploded" up into view. Oblique paralines can also be drawn as "exploded" images with similar characteristics.

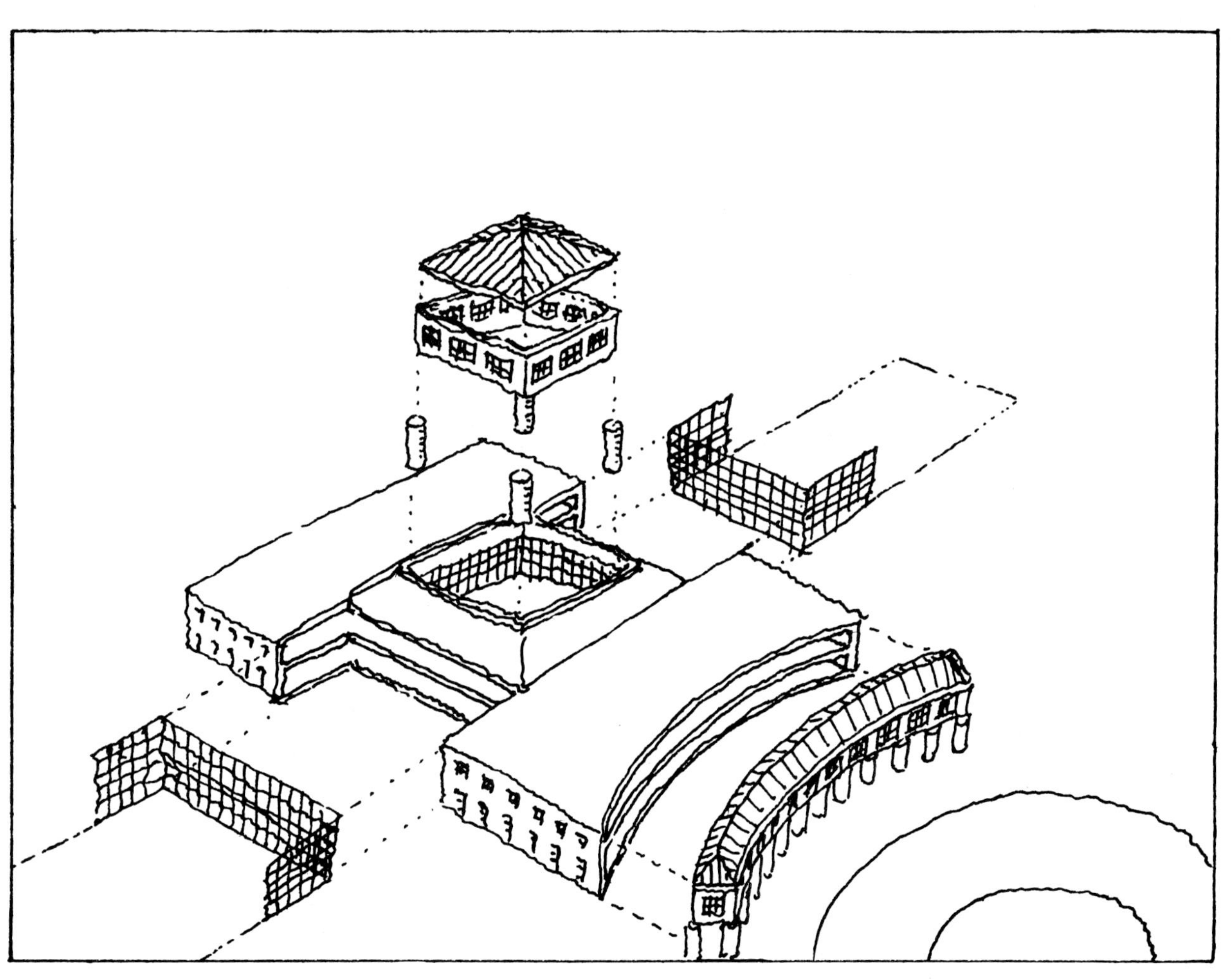

Figure 2.8
Exploded axonometric sketch of an office building in which all the component parts are diagrammed for conceptual clarity.

Figure 2.9
This view of old Paris is traced from the famous "Plan Turgot," demonstrating that paralines are not a new phenomenon. The drawing has been shadowed with black poché used on the horizontal surfaces and hatch on the vertical. Note the segment of the drawing which is left unshaded and the problems of depth perception which occur when shadows are omitted.

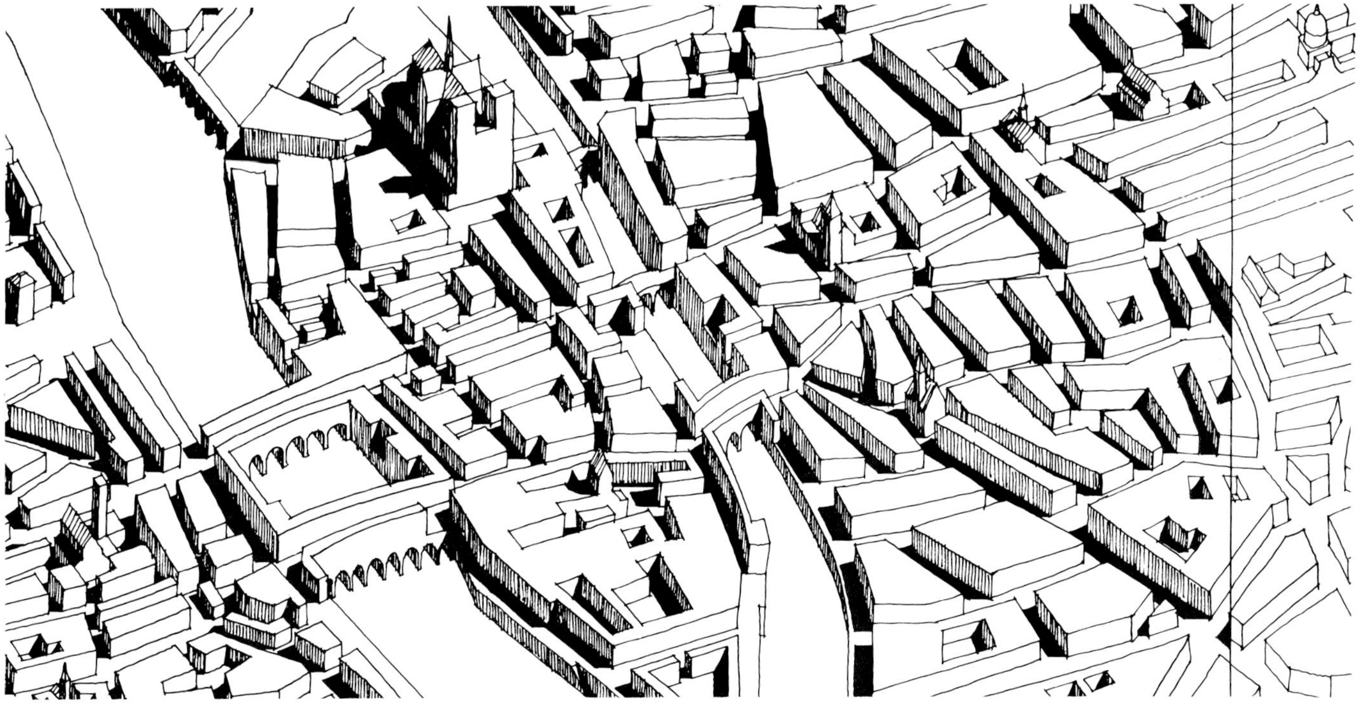

Figure 2.10
Freehand design sketch of a scheme for an urban square.

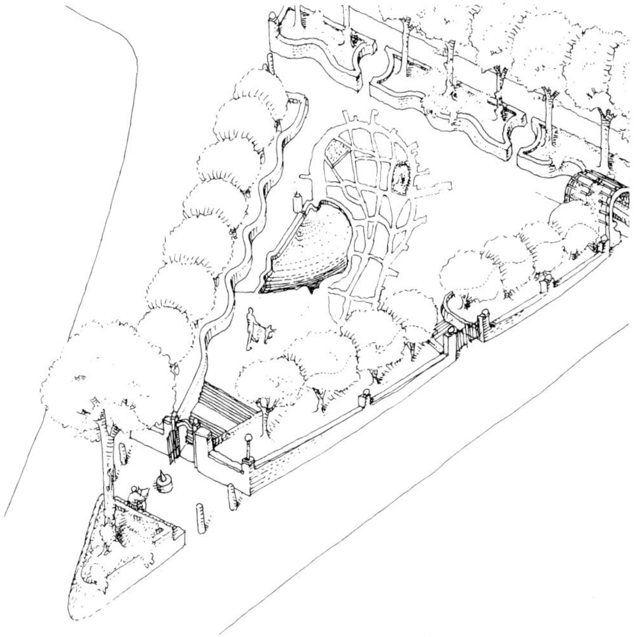

Figure 2.11
Axonometric sketch of an urban housing scheme. Simple shadowing of vertical surfaces and stippling of green spaces help the drawing to "read" spatially.

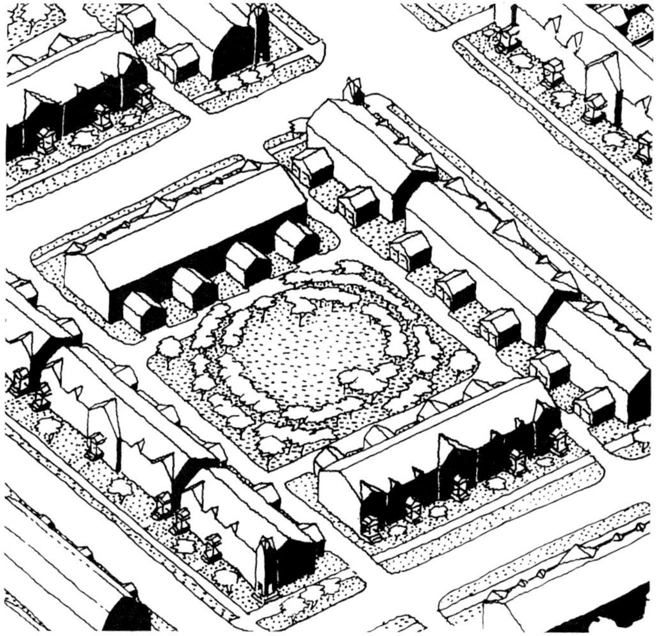

Obliques

There are three types of oblique drawings: cavalier, general, and cabinet. In all three, one principal surface (either the elevation, section, or plan) is drawn true to shape and true to scale. In cavalier obliques, the receding axes are then drawn to full scale. These drawings often appear distorted by the elongation in the receding axes, so other types have been developed. In general obliques, the receding axes are usually foreshortened to three-quarters of full scale, whereas if the receding axes are drawn to half of full scale, the drawing is called a cabinet oblique.

Obliques represent the type of paraline most often used by architects. They offer the distinct advantage of having one principal face of the drawing parallel to the plane of projection, allowing this face to be drawn to true size and scale. Building, site, and roof plans can all be used as the principal plane from which obliques can be constructed. Any complex shapes, circles, ellipses, or arcs can be drawn to their true shape if they are in the principal plane or in a plane parallel to it. This allows obliques to be constructed with relative ease and speed, and makes them useful design tools, as their constituent parts can be more easily developed and altered than in axonometrics. Architects usually draw receding axes at the same scale as the principal plane. This method, although time-saving, tends to make the oblique look artificially elongated. Drawings which require visual accuracy necessitate foreshortening of the receding axes. Many designers feel that foreshortened and visually corrected paralines are difficult to construct, although some simple shortcuts can be used. For example, if a plan oblique is being drawn at a 1/8″ scale, a three-sided scale can be flipped over and receding axes drawn using the 3/32″ side. Similarly with 1/4″ full scale, 3/16″ receding axes can be used. Alternatively, technical illustration manuals will often include foreshortened scales for use in paraline construction. These systems are simple to use and can help produce drawings in which shapes, sizes, and proportions can be studied without severe distortion.

Figure 2.12
Oblique chart demonstrating the basic ways in which cavalier, general, and cabinet drawings can be executed. All images are drawn in cavalier.
A. A true plan oblique, drawn as an up-view. The drawing reveals the mass as seen from below, as well as the plan. Vertical surfaces appear as highly distorted, acute parallelograms.
B. An elevational oblique, drawn as an up-view, shows the mass as seen from below, an undistorted elevation and a view of the distorted plan.
C. A sectional oblique, drawn as an up-view. A true shape section cut can be used to construct this drawing type, with half of the building plan displayed.
D. A down-view, or "bird's-eye," oblique. Perhaps the most often used type of paraline. Mass is well described, and shapes in plan appear true.
E. An elevational oblique, which features a true shape elevation as a picture plan, with all shapes in plan distorted.
F. A sectional oblique drawn as a cut-away, illustrating half of the plan.

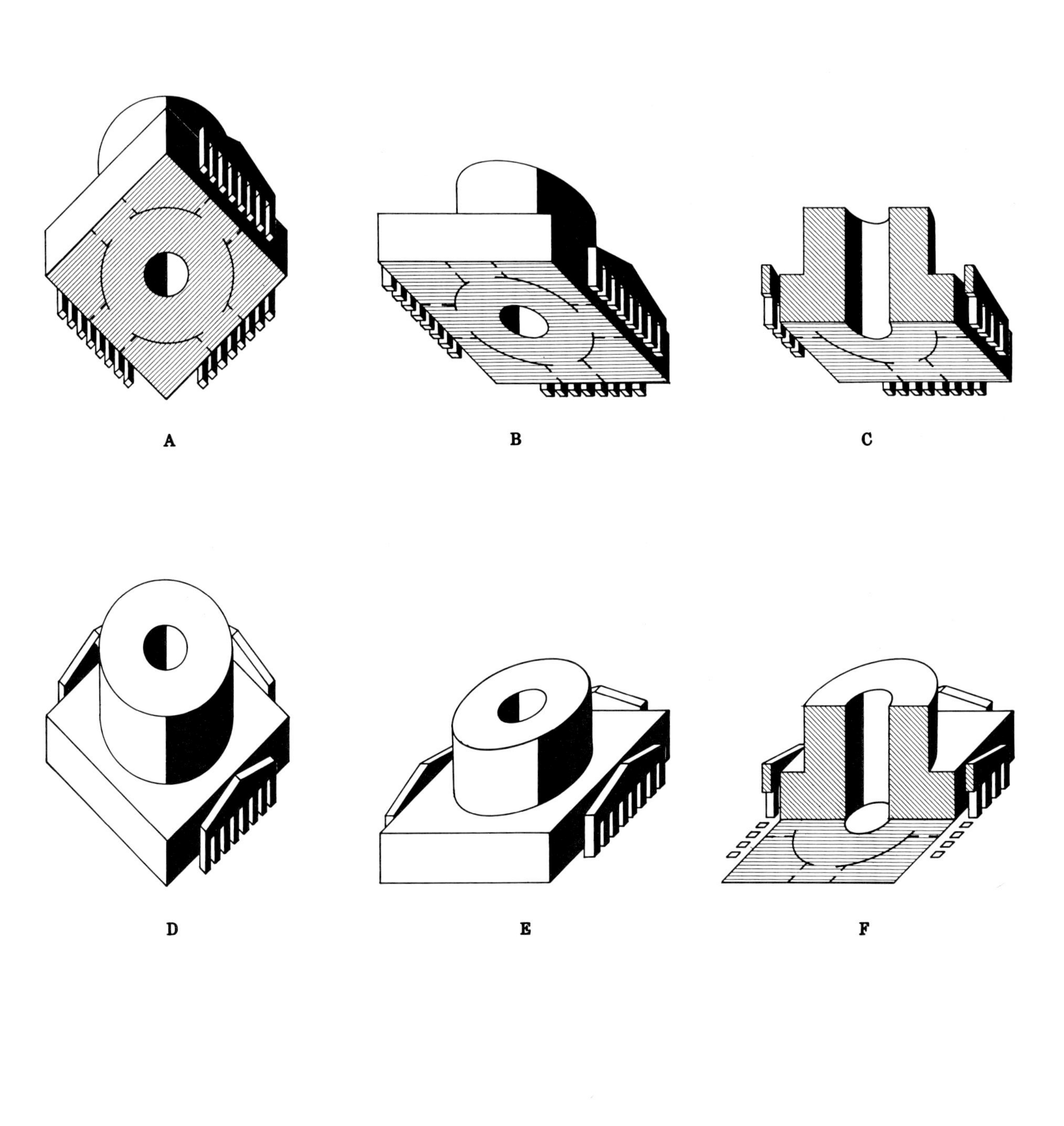

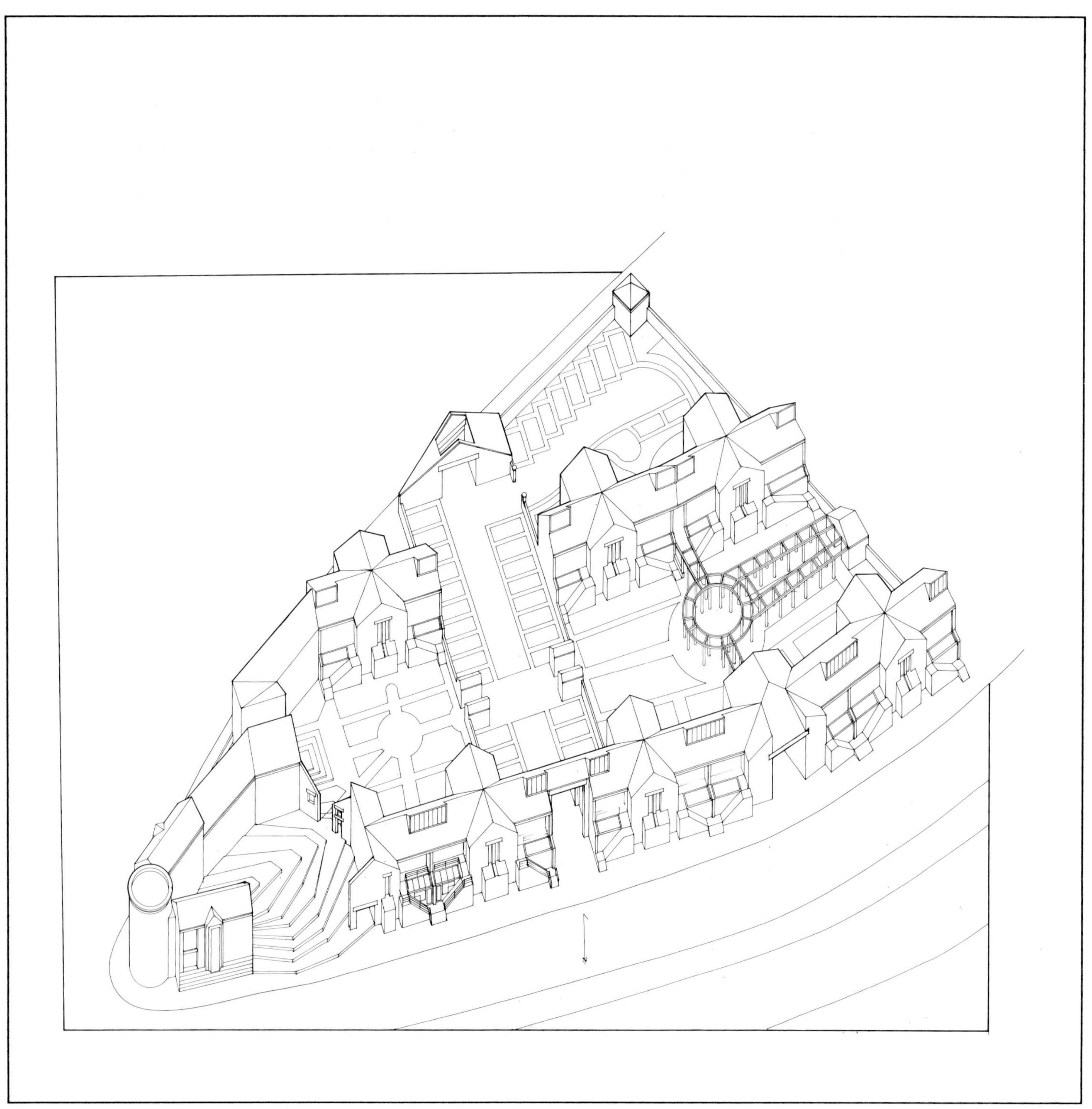

Figure 2.13
A true plan oblique (drawn cavalier) of a housing project for Madison, Wisconsin.

"Up-View" Obliques

Up-view, or "worm's-eye," obliques depict a building or space as if seen from below. These drawings are generally developed around a reverse (or mirrored) plan, wherein facades, interiors, and other elements are constructed with axes receding upward. True elevations or sections can also be used as the primary plane from which up-views are constructed. The up-view oblique can be a useful design tool, enabling the designer to look up into spaces at ceilings, soffits, and wall surfaces which might not be fully illustrated in other drawings.

Figure 2.14
This elevational oblique is drawn as an up-view so that the elements can be studied from a point of view actually experienced by pedestrians. Composed of a series of layers, traditional elevations or down-view paralines were ineffective in describing the facades.

Elevational Obliques

Elevational obliques are a form of paraline drawing which utilize a facade as a principal plane from which elements recede or project. While a principal elevation is presented as a true shape, forms in plan are distorted into parallelograms and can be difficult to understand. This drawing type is useful when elevations are considered as "thick facades" (with depth and/or layers), and effects can be conceived and developed in elevational oblique which would be difficult in simple elevation. When constructed from an aerial viewpoint, these drawings depict a view from a slightly elevated position, perhaps from a nearby hill or building, and thus avoid the extremely elevated "airplane" viewpoints common to plan-generated obliques. It is also possible to construct an elevational oblique from a subterranean viewpoint, which is called an up-view. Whether constructed from aerial or subterranean viewpoints, all elevational obliques require foreshortening of the recession, or depth, scale. If this type of drawing is constructed with only one scale (cavalier), the resulting image will seem artificially elongated. As with other paralines, diagonal elements in plan can appear unusually lengthened or foreshortened.

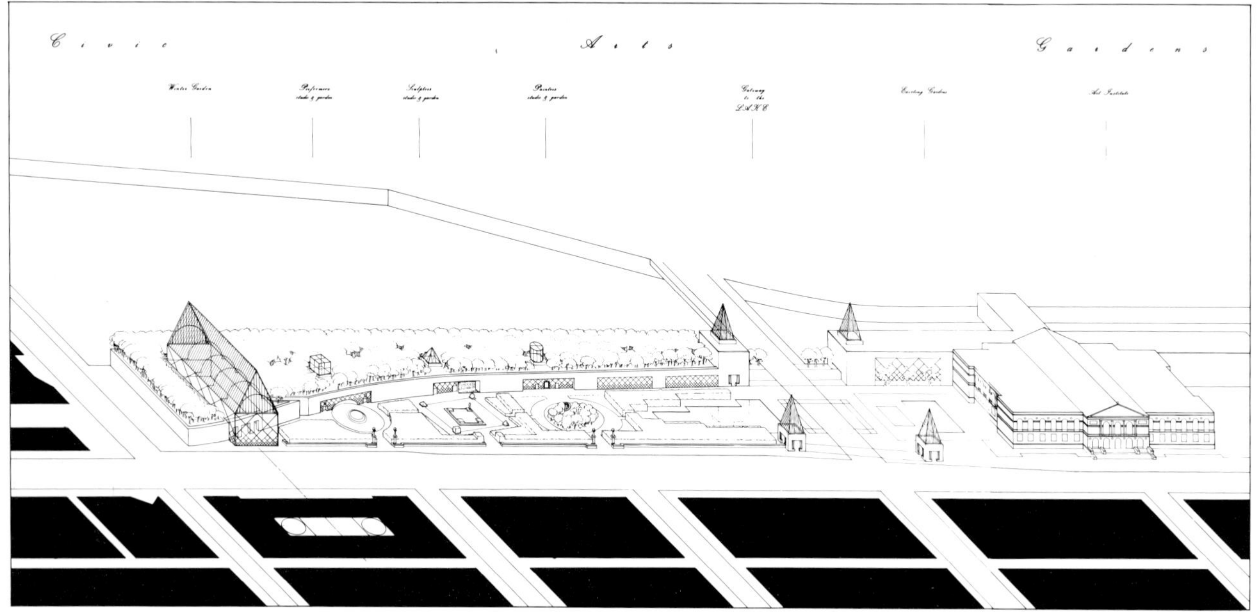

Figure 2.15
The Chicago Architectural Club chose this scheme as first-place winner in a 1984 charrette competition. Constructed as an elevational oblique, the drawing depicts a design for a series of urban gardens near Chicago's Art Institute on Michigan Avenue. Note how the densely built blocks in the foreground are cut-away and pochéd to display the gardens.

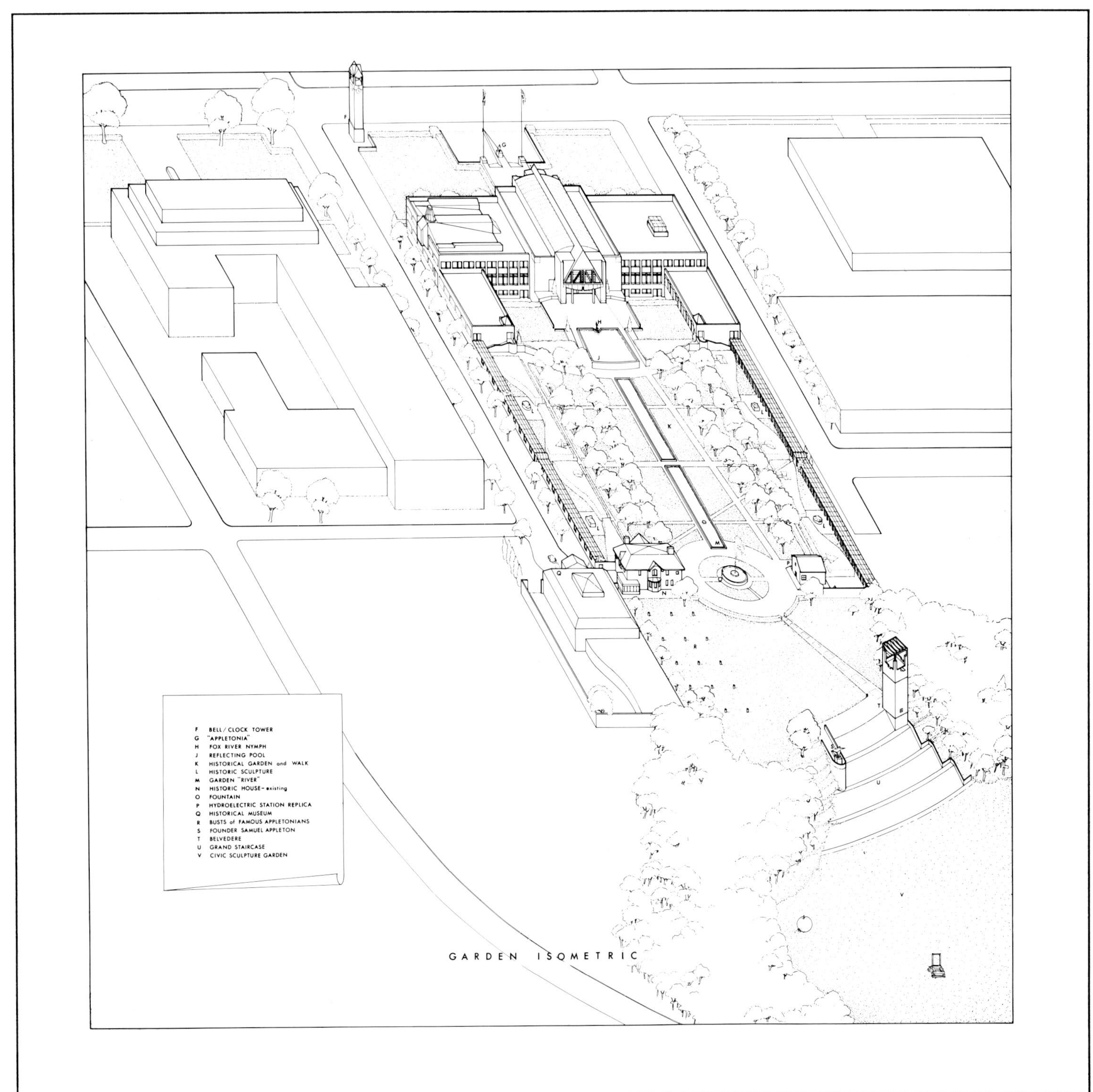

Figure 2.16
An elevational oblique (drawn general) of a scheme for the Appleton, Wisconsin, City Hall and gardens.

True Plan–True Elevation Obliques

Obliques can be drawn which simultaneously depict both plan and elevation as true, undistorted shapes. However, in most circumstances the drawings appear flat, and they are generally considered difficult to understand. Familiarity can, of course, reduce these problems, although clients and laymen may find them unclear. Both true plan and true elevation tend to resemble parts of a model that have yet to be folded and assembled. Certain kinds of designs, however, do lend themselves to these drawings. For example, designs with grid shifts tend to work well, as the "shifted" parts appear in regular oblique while the advantages of both true plan and true elevation construction are maintained. Furthermore, these drawings can attain a static, abstract quality, as the drawing can be composed entirely of "true" shapes, lacking the distorted effects typical of other paralines.

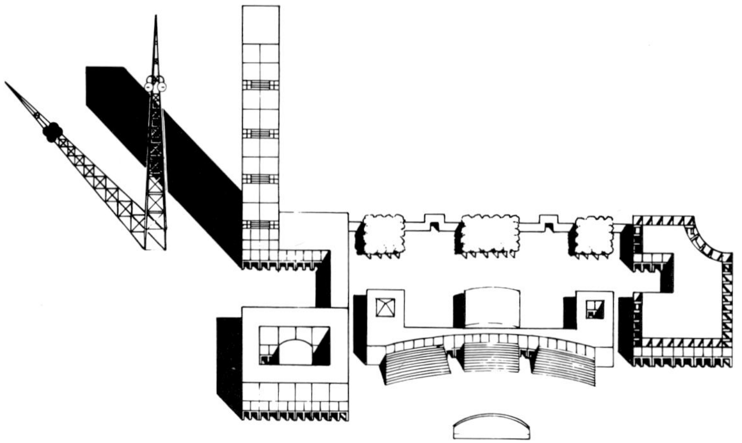

Figure 2.17
This true plan, true elevation oblique, represents a study for a major cultural center in New Delhi, India. The drawing has received cast shadows, which helps an otherwise "flat" drawing to be read spatially. Composed entirely of true shapes, the drawing is simple to execute and exhibits a static, stable quality.

Sectional Obliques

Similar in many ways to section perspectives, sectional obliques use a true-shaped section cut as picture plane, from which elements recede in oblique. The drawing type is best utilized to study and present major rooms and spaces.

Images of squares, streets, courts, atria, etc. can be quickly generated from sections and used as design tools to visualize the relationship between section and the quality of space. Sectional obliques are easier to construct than section perspectives, primarily because all elements can be drawn to scale. Section perspectives can, however, reveal five surfaces (three walls, ceiling, and floor) of a rectangular room, while oblique views show only three surfaces. Sectional obliques can also be drawn as up-views and should always be drawn with foreshortened depth scales.

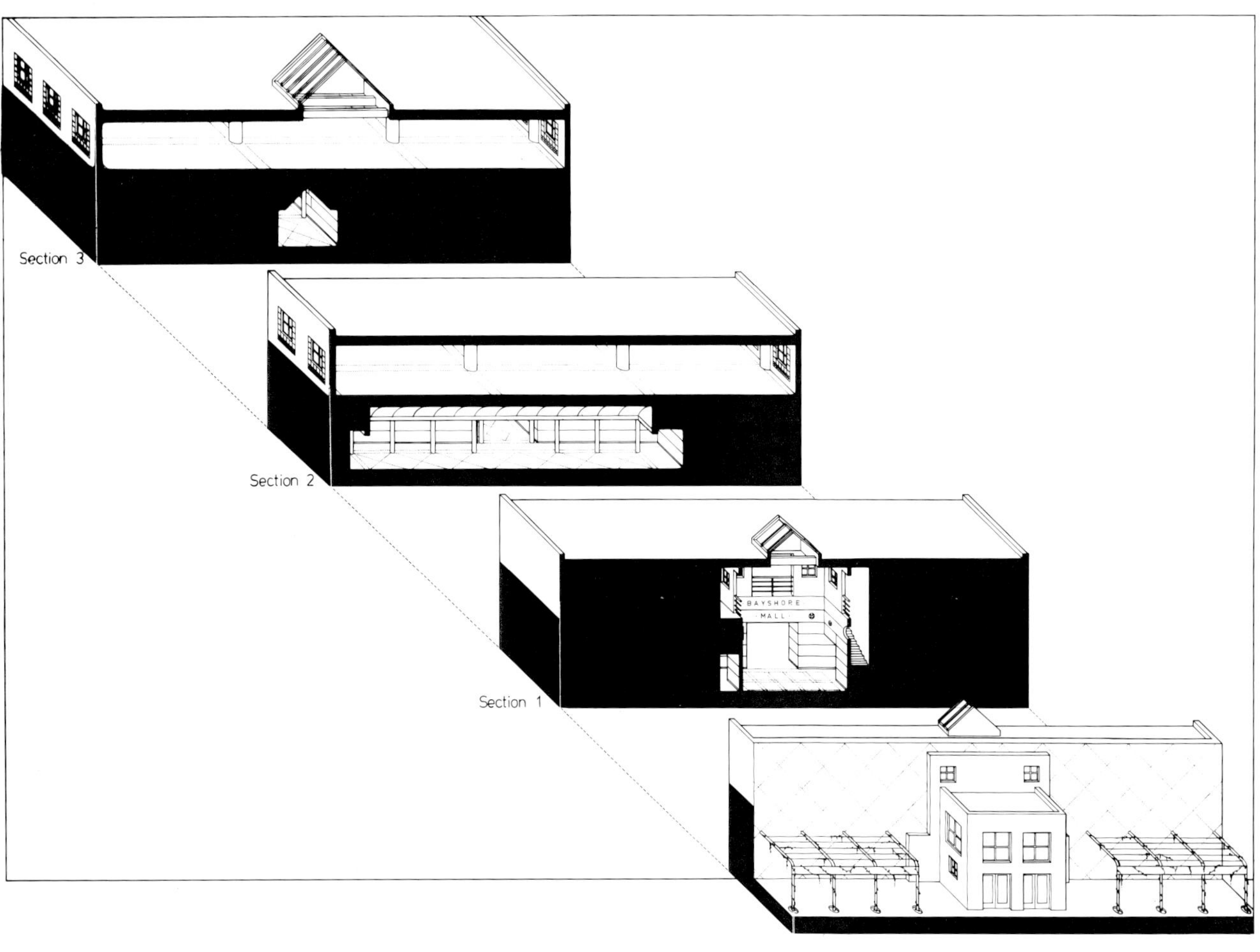

Figure 2.18
Elevational and sectional obliques are combined in this exploded drawing of a retail mall with upper-level office space. Drawn as a series of slices, each image depicts an architectural event in the sequence in which a pedestrian would encounter it.

Figure 2.19
Proposed renovations to this Victorian house were designed and developed in the form of an elevational oblique. The drawing displays a relatively low point of view, with undistorted elements in elevation. These characteristics make the drawing type ideal for the study of frontal, street-edge buildings.

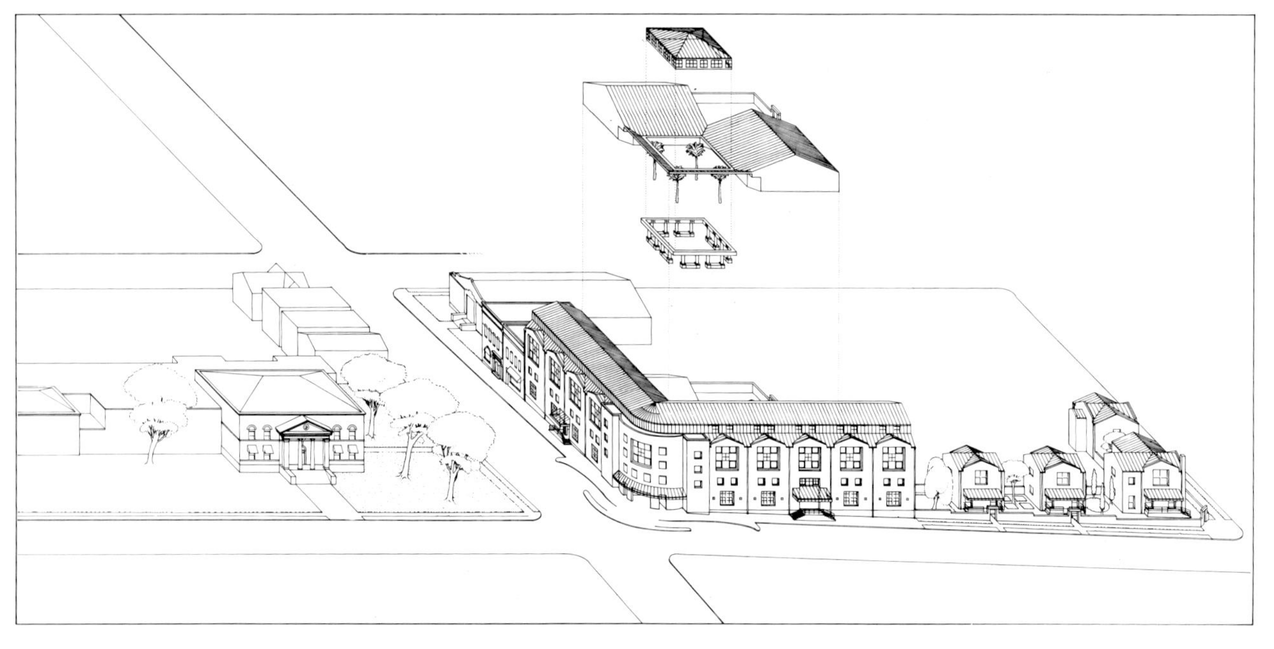

Figure 2.20
A project for a resort hotel is drawn as an exploded elevational oblique (drawn general). The single-story atrium and service buildings, which would be hidden in a typical view, are "exploded" up into view.

Chapter Three
Perspective Drawing

Although perspective drawing as a technique is fairly commonplace in the contemporary presentation process, its original development had a considerable impact in the fields of art, architecture, and science. In the fifteenth century, the concept of perspective represented a new way of thinking about space and provided an entirely new method for observing and recording the world. By virtue of its realistic viewpoint, the perspective placed the viewer at the center of the field of vision, manipulating space and form to respond with geometric precision to the eye of the audience. As such, perspective drawing ordered and organized space with Renaissance Man as its prime focus.

The first to publish an organized treatise describing a practical method for employing perspective was Leon Battista Alberti. His work concerned both painting and architecture and, in fact, advised against the use of perspective in architectural representation. Since then, the use of perspective in architecture has been questioned, debated, and qualified, and designers have extolled its virtues or condemned its distortions. To understand perspective drawing better, therefore, a brief examination of its advantages and shortcomings may be useful.

Perhaps more than any other graphic device, perspective pictorial projections are capable of representing three-dimensional reality on a flat sheet of paper. Both architects and laymen, conditioned by photographic and televisual images, can usually understand perspectives more readily than other kinds of drawings. The effect is obtained by collectively representing the phenomena of foreshortening, convergence and distortion that the human eye sees when observing the built world. This effect, however, is obtained at the expense of distorting "true" architectural measurements and proportions, which was seen by some Renaissance designers as a principal shortcoming of perspective drawing.

Although they can convey some spatial characteristics convincingly, perspectives are not as optically real as they may seem. For example, basic perspectives cannot deal with the observed phenomenon of the curving of straight lines as seen in peripheral vision. Other shortcomings have been observed which must to some degree temper a designer's trust in perspectives as a "true and objective" medium of spatial depiction.

Figure 3.1
An eye-level perspective view of a proposed streetscape treatment for the main street of Shorewood, Wisconsin.

LEONARDO'S PARADOX

Leonardo da Vinci was among the first to recognize the limitations of normal artificial perspective, and the classic demonstration of perspective distortion is known as "Leonardo's paradox." Here, the observer is placed in front of an evenly spaced row of columns. As the eye looks directly at the row, the column width appears to diminish as the columns get farther away from the viewer. If, however, a one-point perspective drawing is constructed of the scene with the picture plane parallel to the row of columns, it can be observed that the constructed widths of the columns will appear larger as they get farther away, while their heights remain the same. The drawing therefore describes images which are in direct conflict with the observer's actual experience, and the principal depth clues that would allow the drawing to be "read" (i.e., diminishing column width and height) are not present in the perspective construction to aid the viewer's comprehension.

While these effects are most readily seen in a row of columns, any one-point perspective drawing contains similar distortions, even if there are no elements which make them readily apparent. Distortions are most severe in views with wide angles of vision, although it is possible to limit distortions by keeping narrow vision angles. (In fact, Leonardo suggested a field of vision of as little as 20 degrees, which seems excessively cautious).

It is also possible, although somewhat impractical, to allow drawings to be seen monocularly from one precise spectator point. Written instructions for viewing can be provided, or a shadow box can be constructed which can be used to ensure the viewer has only a limited range of vision when viewing the drawing. When seen from their correctly constructed spectator point, perspective drawings can appear very realistic, and construction distortions are minimized. Such a system has obvious shortcomings in the presentation of drawings, although the opportunities are intriguing and may in some instances be worth investigating.

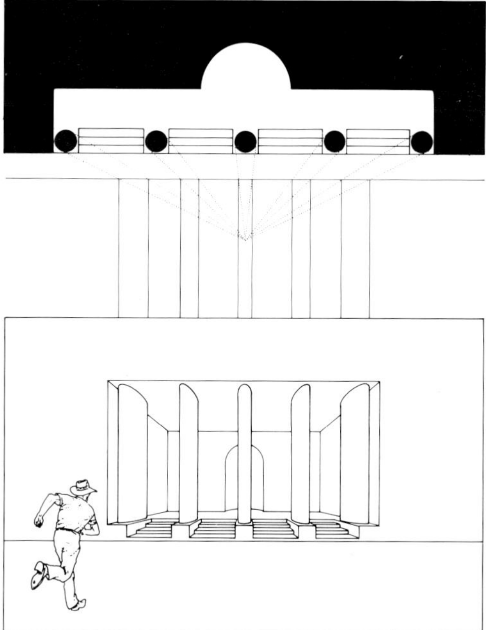

Figure 3.2
In this wide angle-of-vision one-point perspective, the severe distortions known as "Leonardo's paradox" can be observed. Note especially how columns which are closest to the viewer seem the smallest in diameter, while those farthest away grow wide—exactly the reverse of the phenomenon that would actually be observed.

THE SINGULAR AND STATIONARY POINT OF VIEW

Typically, both one- and two-point perspectives assume a single, stationary point of view. While considered adequate for most situations, this construction has certain limitations which were recognized by Leonardo da Vinci and Raphael. Among these limitations is the stationary nature of perspective images. In reality, the viewer constantly alters the position of the body and head to gather cumulative information about a space. The inability of stationary perspective drawing to deal with the actual, dynamic perception of space is a principal limitation of the convention. To draw a single perspective, and to make design decisions based upon it as a true representation of space, may be misleading both to the audience and to the designer.

These problems have sometimes led architects to abandon the use of perspectives. Raphael, for example, rejected the idea of a single vantage point for the viewer and experimented with multiple vantage points in a single drawing to give the perspective the effects of "real" perception. He found one- and two-point perspectives virtually incapable of de-

Figure 3.3
The Temple of Love in the Gardens in Chantilly. The central pavilion is carefully drawn with considerable detail, while peripheral elements in the drawing have been quickly drawn, lacking detail. This is an old drawing technique, which mirrors the nature of human vision.

Figure 3.4
A sketch of Laon Cathedral looking east down the nave.

picting certain spaces (curved interiors, for example) and worked on developing a drawing type suited to his vision of space.

However, the stationary nature of perspective drawing can be considered an advantage when applied to certain situations. The spectacular Olympic Theatre in Vicenza, for example, was designed to take unique advantage of the audience's stationary viewpoint. The illusion of deep space is created by artificially foreshortening "buildings" and "streets" of plaster and wood, creating a powerful and realistic three-dimensional effect.

Similarly, it has been proposed that many Greek sites (the Acropolis among them) were planned to be experienced from a few specific vantage points. An entrance gateway would be chosen, for example, and all buildings and architectural elements would be distributed to appear harmonious from this singular spectator point. Controlling the viewpoint can therefore present a powerful image to an audience and can be a useful presentation tool for designers seeking to impress or persuade.

BOUNDED AND ENCLOSED SPACE

Early in the twentieth century, certain artists and designers suggested that perspective was more than a drawing method and that it represented a way of seeing and designing space which was alien to their new ideas and sensibilities. For example, the constructivist El Lissitzki wrote:

> Perspective bounded and enclosed space, but science has since brought about a fundamental revision. The rigidity of Euclidian space has been annihilated. . . .

Thus, modern architects' desire for boundless, universal, and nonaxial space made the perspective a tool unsuitable for the depiction of these ideas.

For many of these modern architects, the perspective was not the "neutral" drawing device it tends to be regarded as today. Architects and painters such as El Lissitzki saw it as loaded with ideological bias, suited for depicting contained and axial volumes of space and intended to be seen from unique and central vantage points. This idea of perspective as a "symbolic form" of representation is significant in the light of the current examination of "classical" systems in architectural design. For example, axial symmetry, the architectural promenade, and space as discrete and enclosed figures are concepts which in recent years have seen a revival of interest. As architectural ideology shifts closer to those effects which are perhaps best portrayed with perspective drawing, it is desirable that such drawings take their place as an integral element of the design process.

Figure 3.5
A view of the vast garden vista at Vaux-le-Vicomte, as seen from the upper terrace level. Note how masses of many trees and complex parterre patterns are simplified into simple shapes.

A POSTERIORI USE

Perspective drawing is typically treated by the profession today as an "after the fact" examination of a design which has usually been planned with other drawing types. It tends to be regarded as a drawing intended primarily for the client or other audience, while the more conventional vehicles of plans, sections, and paralines are used more as professional tools in design generation. In fact, many perspectives of buildings are prepared not by the designer, but by a hired illustrator who takes other drawings (or a model) and prepares what is essentially a surrogate for a photograph. Although these drawings are often the most effective image that lay people can understand, some architects have exhibited indifference or disdain for the rendered perspective.

However, many prominent designers have perceived perspectives as an integral part of the design process and have used them in their earliest project sketches. Such diverse figures as Bramante and Frank Lloyd Wright, for example, both made extensive use of perspective drawing throughout their design work and did not reserve them for use solely in the presentation process. Even today, other design fields such as industrial design or scenography make considerable and significant use of perspective drawing in design.

Theatrical designer Tim Palkovic expressed a commonly held viewpoint when he wrote:

> The most desirable approach to design drawing begins with a perspective sketch that is easily translated into a floor plan. This insures that perceptual problems are considered from the conception of the design and not discovered later.

Although the stationary position of the audience in a theatre makes it easier to apply perspective to scenography than to architectural design, architects should be aware of the advantages of this attitude, as the perspective offers the only route to study in drawn form the way in which a space will actually look to a person located within it.

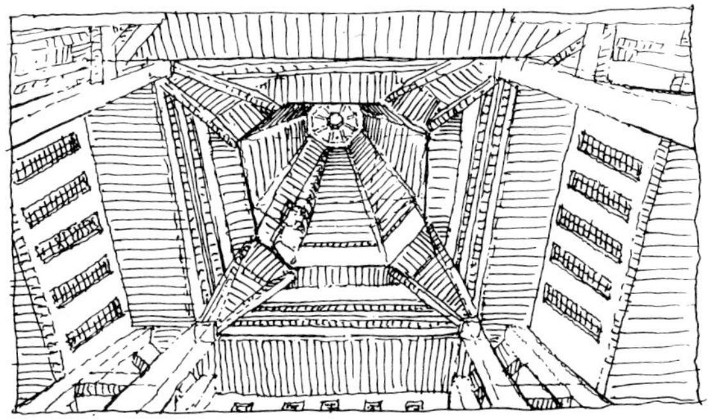

Figure 3.6
Auguste Perret's concrete cathedral at Le Havre viewed looking up into the light tower. The sketch is actually a two-point perspective, with one vanishing point at the zenith. Views looking up at tall objects are often experienced but seldom drawn by architects.

ONE-POINT (PARALLEL) PERSPECTIVES

The first type of perspective construction to be developed, and one which was widely used during the Renaissance era, was the one-point, or parallel, perspective. By far the simplest perspective type to construct, the one-point utilizes a true-shape orthographic plane. Like oblique paraline drawings, it is the true-shape plane that can be used to make one-point perspectives simple to develop and use. For example, if the picture plane is placed at a known elevation, the features of that plane can be drawn true to shape at the scale of the generating plan.

This plane then serves as the basis around which the entire drawing can be constructed, with all elements receding and advancing from it. The ease of construction allows this type of drawing to be used during the design process, instead of strictly as a presentation tool.

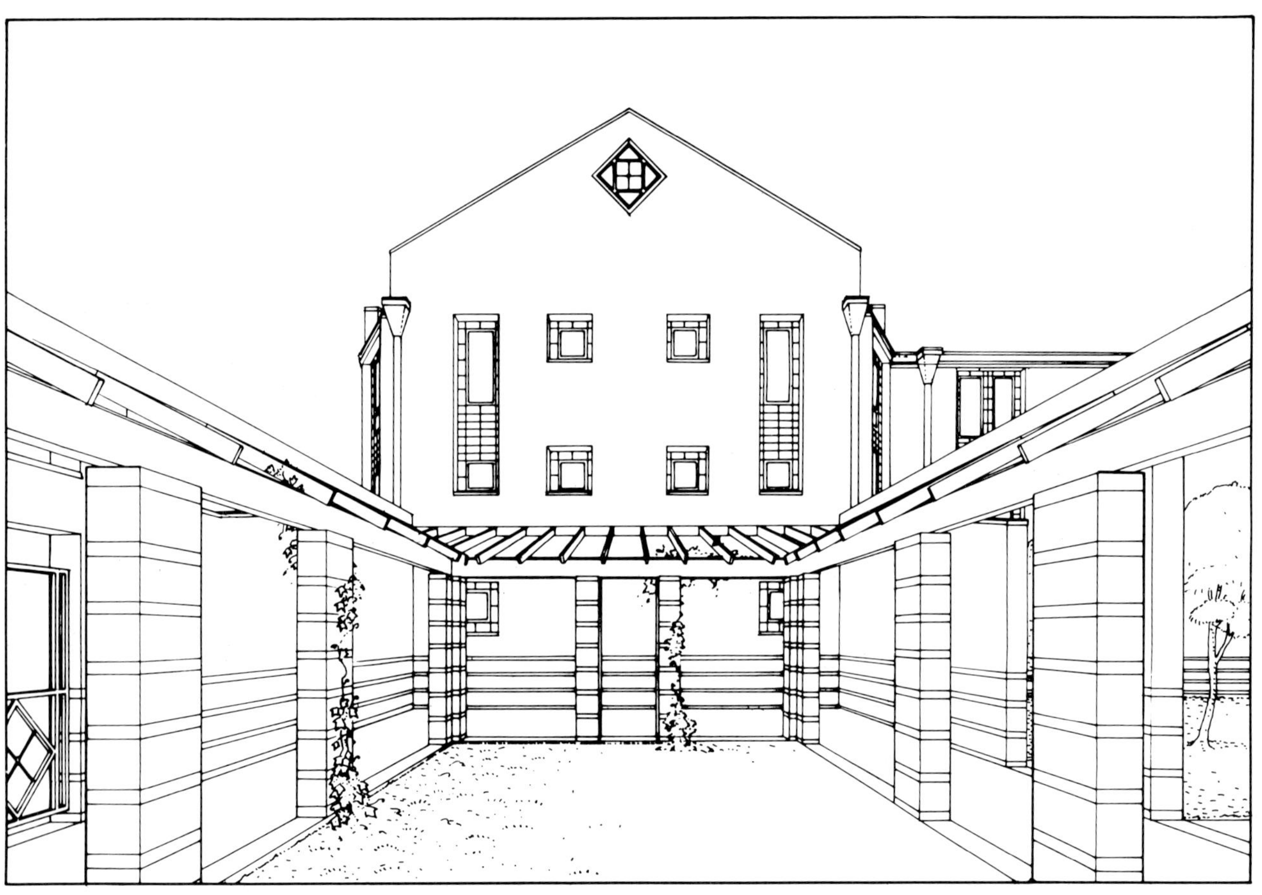

Figure 3.7
One-point perspective view of a cloistered courtyard adjoining the Merit Hall dormitory on the University of Wisconsin/Madison campus. The conventions of the one-point were well suited to depict the static, enclosed, symmetrical court. Although the view was constructed from a plan, the picture plane was located so that a previously constructed elevation could be traced. (Compare with Figure 3.13.)

The placement of the picture plane parallel to a major surface often lends these drawings an air of frontality and formality, which can affect the way in which the design is perceived. Leonardo da Vinci undertook significant research into perspective theory and use and was ultimately disillusioned with the "harmonic boxes" which seemed to be the outcome of this system.

It has been argued with some validity that designing within the one-point perspective system produces a theatrical conception of space and encourages the design of simple cubical rooms arranged with axial symmetry. As a drawing type, therefore, one-point perspectives are ideally suited to depict buildings which are composed and experienced axially and frontally. Alternatively, they may be used serially or in conjunction with other drawing types to explore space and form in a way which does not limit or distort the designer's understanding of the design which is being created.

Figure 3.8
The stair and dining hall of a summer home was drawn as a one-point, from the exact position from which the hall is first entered. The clerestory windows are placed in false perspective (as are the stairs) in order to increase the apparent size of the small hall from this point of view. Design decisions made in the perspective view were later recorded in plan and section.

Figure 3.9
Porch of the summer home, overlooking Big Green Lake. A serene and quiet-looking figure has been drawn in to help create an atmosphere of tranquility and repose.

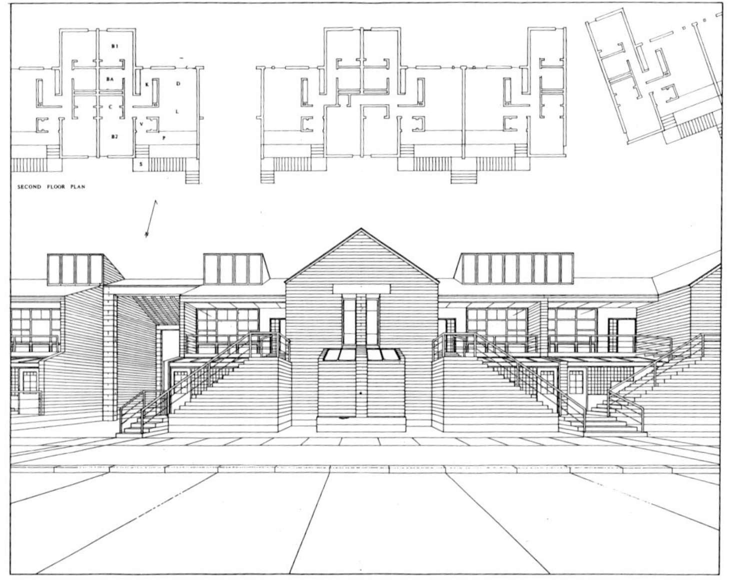

Figure 3.10
A one-point perspective of a multi-family housing project in Madison, Wisconsin. The plan from which the view was constructed is drawn in a light pen weight "floating" above the perspective, which allows direct comparison of the two views.

Figure 3.11
This enclosed, axial courtyard has been drawn as a one-point, focusing on a distant vista of the Wisconsin State Capitol. A photograph of the Capitol, taken from the site, has been pasted into the drawing. The plan used in the construction of the perspective has been drawn as a framed figure ground, hovering in the sky above the view.

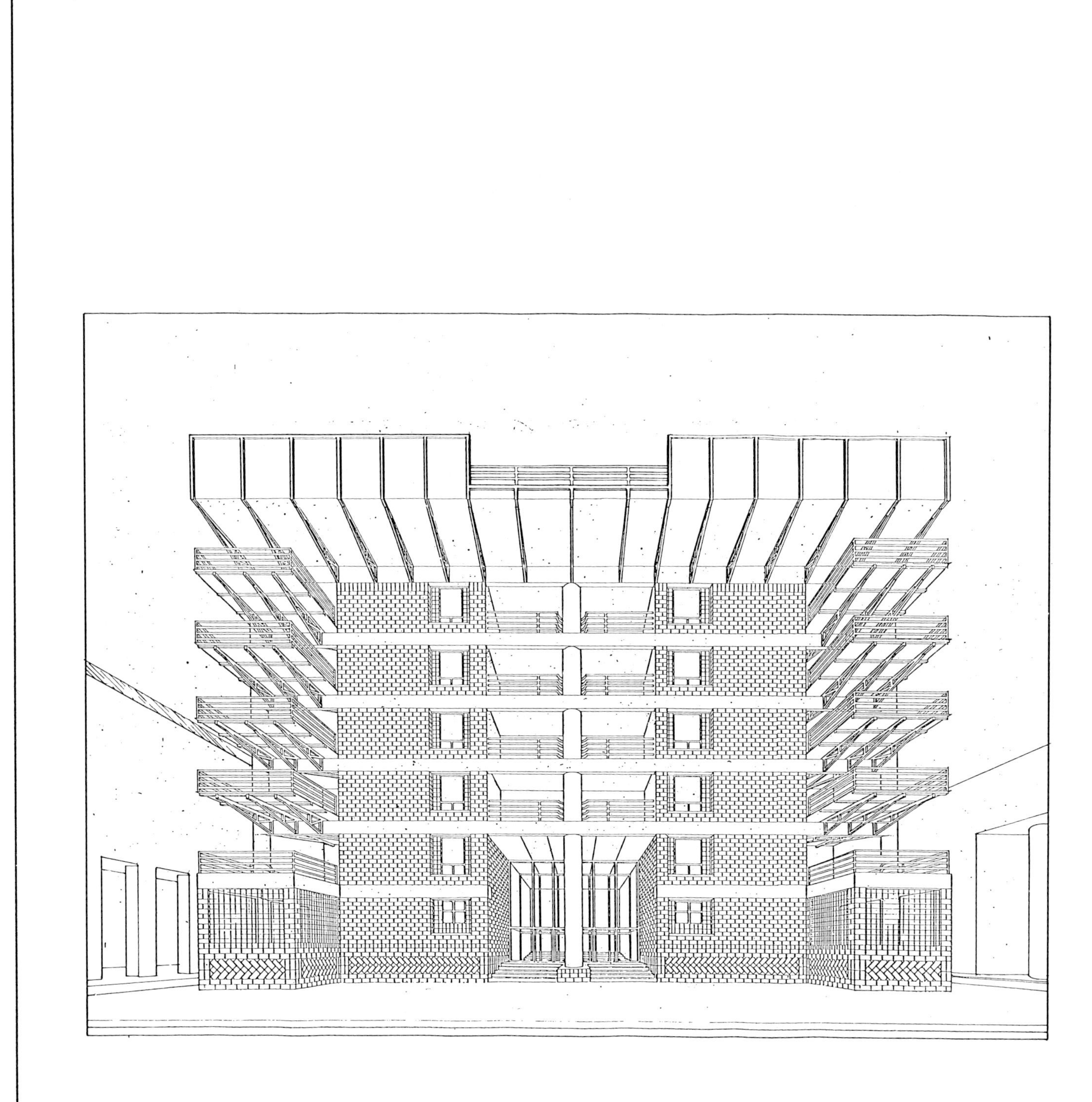

Figure 3.12
The principal facade of an apartment block has been drawn as a one-point, which was generated from an elevation drawn to scale. This procedure included the use of photocopied concrete block texture which was cut and pasted into place, reducing the drawing time.

TWO-POINT (ANGULAR) PERSPECTIVES

Two-point perspectives are generally acknowledged to be the most "realistic" type of projection drawing, as they are able to depict spaces and buildings more convincingly than one-point perspectives. "True" visual perception is represented by the recession of all horizontal lines to their respective vanishing points, whereas in the one-point perspective, one primary plane retains its exact shape. As the word "angular" would imply, the nature of two-point images is the dynamic and diagonal point of view. Buildings which are intended to be seen obliquely, as well as spaces which are intended to be experienced diagonally, are best depicted in two-point drawings.

These qualifications are broad, however, and the two-point system is so versatile that an experienced designer can adapt the convention to most requirements. The "realism" of two-point perspectives is derived at the expense of increased difficulty of construction, as these drawings require more time, skill, and technical knowledge than other drawing types, which can tend to limit their effectiveness in the design process.

Figure 3.13
Two-point perspective view of the street corner entry to the Merit Hall dormitory on the University of Wisconsin/Madison campus. The conventions of the two-point were well suited to describe the diagonal entry axis into the corner pavilion. (Compare with Figure 3.7.)

Figure 3.14
This two-point was used during the schematic design of a housing complex in Milwaukee, Wisconsin. The basic masses were accurately constructed, so that the drawing could be used to sketch fenestration alternatives as they would be seen from a nearby public square.

Figure 3.15
A carefully constructed two-point perspective of a harborfront building shows the massing of the scheme. By giving more emphasis to one elevation, however, a great deal of facade detail can be included.

CURVED PICTURE PLANE PERSPECTIVES

The distortions of typical perspective drawings have long troubled some designers, and attempts have been made to develop systems to correct the distortions perceived in Leonardo's paradox. One approach is the use of a curved picture plane, which might be compared to a glass cylinder about the viewer's head. Images are recorded on this curved plane, which is then rolled back onto a flat surface. The images thus constructed can appear to agree more closely with normal visual experience, especially at the edges of wide angle-of-vision views. However, there are complications. If this method is followed carefully, all lines at right angles to the viewer's principal line of sight must be drawn as curved lines. This, of course, enormously complicates construction and in some instances can lend an impression of distortion which is more disturbing than the problems which were originally intended to be corrected.

Figure 3.16
The markets at London's Covent Garden are sketched here in a curved picture plane perspective. The sketch accurately records the experience of standing in a single position while turning one's head from left to right, looking up and down the street edge. A true section of the same markets is drawn above the perspective.

SECTION PERSPECTIVES

Section perspective drawings date back to the early Renaissance, and designers such as Leonardo and Bramante used them, primarily to describe buildings with centralized interior spaces. These drawings have the ability to present all of the information found in a building section, adding to it a convincing depiction of the volume of space contained within. Beginning with a "true" section shape, section perspectives are perhaps the simplest of all perspectives to construct. While they are usually simple one-point drawings, designers may make the mistake of not using a plan layout to construct the image, instead estimating the depth of recession. The result can be drawings that are badly distorted and therefore of limited usefulness in the design process.

Section perspectives are used principally to study major interior spaces or enclosed courts, streets, and squares. Such drawings are a valuable presentation tool, as laymen can usually "read" them more readily than simple sections. They are also a useful design tool, allowing architects to make decisions relatively quickly in perspective, while being able to immediately see and record their impact on the section. Section perspectives, however, generally have the effect of removing the spectator from any intimacy with the scene being drawn by virtue of the abstract nature of the sectional cut.

Although they lack the ability to place the viewer inside a space, they do present more information about a building than standard perspective drawings. They can show several spaces simultaneously and describe their horizontal and vertical interconnections. Usually, a single vanishing point is placed at eye level within a major space. Multiple vanishing points can be placed in a single section, although the results are usually disconcerting and the overall visual result may be abstract and confusing rather than clarifying.

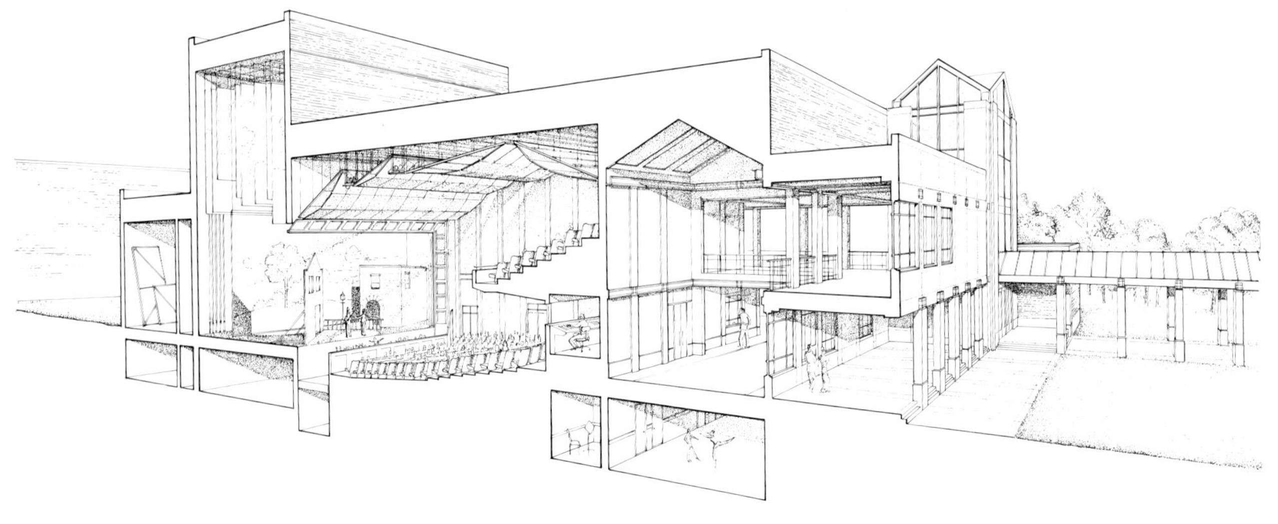

Figure 3.17
By placing the vanishing point outside the building, this section perspective can describe the exterior mass and surfaces of a theatre while at the same time revealing the character of the major interiors.

PLAN PERSPECTIVES

Plan perspectives are a composite drawing type, combining the abstract information of a plan view with the spatial depiction of a perspective. Typically, a true plan is used as a base drawing, and then a one-point "bird's-eye" perspective is constructed, with the vanishing point placed in the most important space. A section or elevation can be used to develop both spectator point and picture plane, enabling the construction of an accurate depth of recession. Usually, however, designers simply estimate the recession depth.

These drawings are very useful for presentation purposes, as they provide multiple layers of information in a comprehensible, singular format. Other types of plan perspectives can be used to the same effect, such as plans seen as "cut-aways" from eye level or from slightly elevated positions (as if viewing a building under construction). Frank Lloyd Wright often made use of these techniques while designing, although the distortions and construction difficulties involved tend to limit their usefulness.

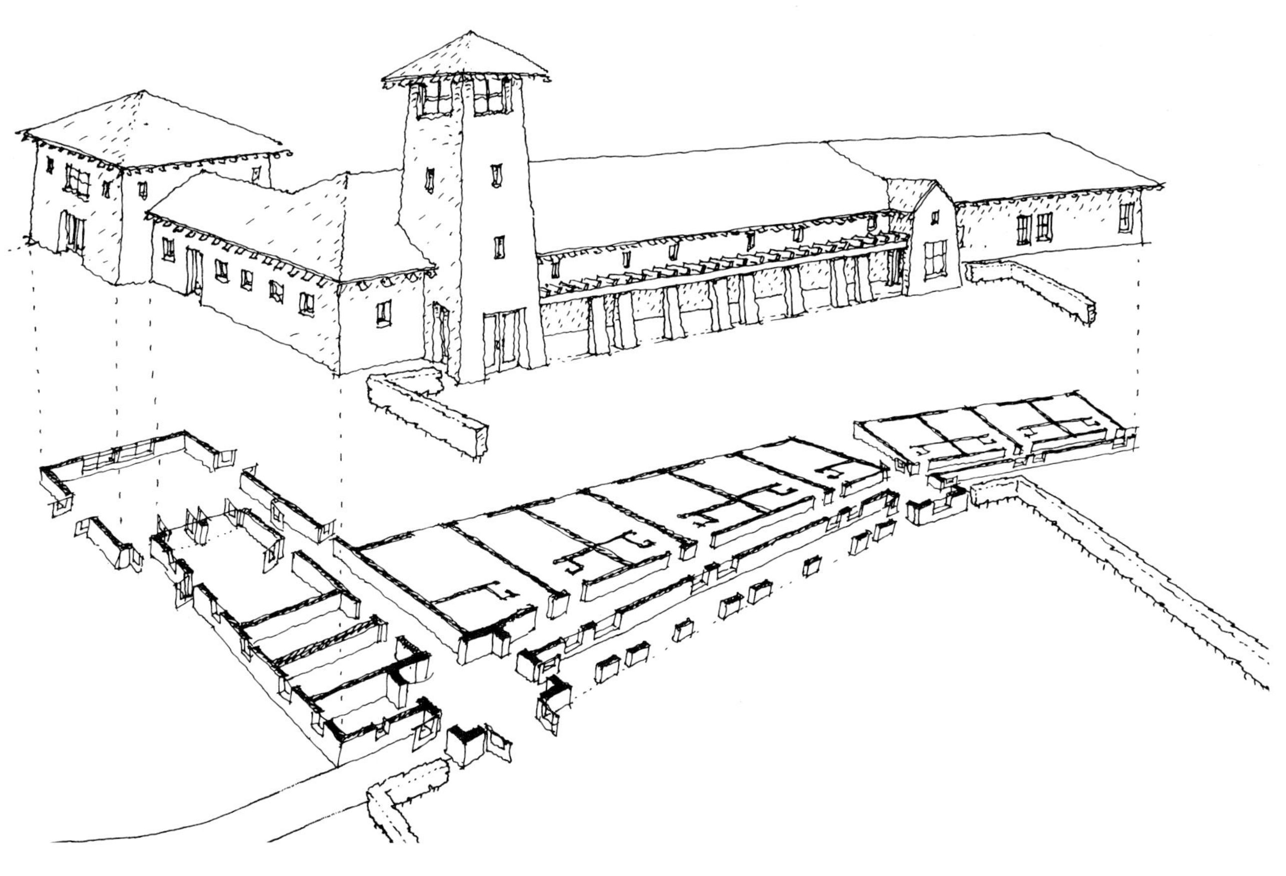

Figure 3.18
A schematic design for a religious retreat has been drawn as a plan perspective, in which the mass of the building is shown hovering above a cut-away plan.

THE BIRD'S-EYE VIEW

The convention of the bird's-eye perspective is claimed to have been introduced into architectural drawing by Leonardo da Vinci, who used views throughout his sketch books for a wide variety of purposes. The drawings have the distinct advantage of being able to present complex information regarding the three-dimensional form of an object in a single view. They utilize a high and distant vantage point, allowing two sides and the top of any cubical solid to be seen simultaneously. Although they resemble axonometrics or obliques (depending upon the chosen vantage point), bird's-eye perspectives are more difficult to construct than paralines and, like all perspectives, can be a difficult medium in which to design. If the difficulties of construction can be overcome, however, the bird's-eye perspective can achieve more realistic and less distorted images than paralines. Of course, the high point of view which can reveal the structure in its entirety also has a tendency to remove the observer to a distant and abstract vantage point. Scale and detailed information are generally sacrificed for conceptual information, as the building is being shown from a viewpoint that may rarely, if ever, be encountered. Although they are well suited to holistically depict complex objects, they tend to lack detail and scale from a realistic viewpoint, and in this way tend to resemble axonometrics and obliques. However, if used in conjunction with other drawing types, the bird's-eye perspective can be a powerful communication tool.

Figure 3.19 (at left)
A bird's-eye perspective sketch was used to record the existing condition of North Square, in Boston.

Figure 3.20 (at right)
Schematic design alternatives for a history museum and urban landscape improvements were developed in the form of a bird's-eye sketch, utilizing Figure 3.19 as a base sketch for tracing-paper overlays.

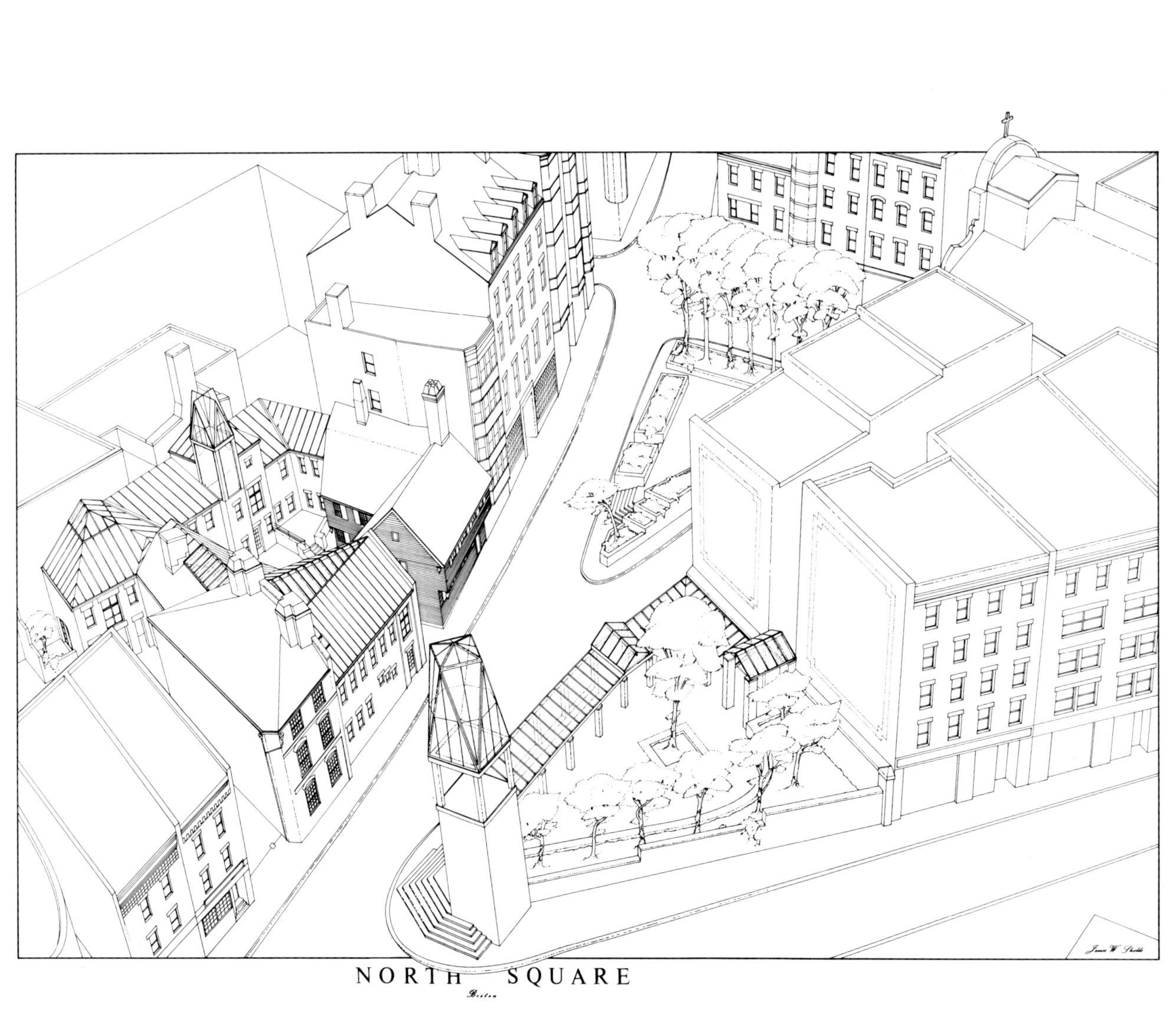

Figure 3.21
An ink hardline drawing of the final scheme for North Square, presented in the form of a bird's-eye perspective.

SERIAL VISION DRAWINGS

The inability of a single, stationary perspective drawing to describe the dynamic and cumulative experience of space is often cited as its principal limitation. A technique of using multiple drawings, generally referred to as "serial vision," has been developed to deal with this problem. These drawings involve the construction of several images which, when viewed in a specific order, give a cumulative impression of actual movement through a spatial sequence. Ideally, the images would flow smoothly into one another, rather like cartoon animation, although generally, serial vision drawings depict an image of each major spatial change along an axis or promenade. Serial drawings of a building, for example, might show the gateway, forecourt, portico, vestibule, and stairhall, all in sequential order, with each drawing implying the next. While serial vision drawings are generally used for presentation purposes, they have some value as design drawings, if they can be quickly and accurately generated early in the design process.

Figure 3.22
These sketches (courtesy of Beckley/Myers Architects) depict Milwaukee's theatre district in the form of six serial vision perspectives.

NONCONSTRUCTED PERSPECTIVES

In some cases, the process of construction of a perspective drawing may be avoided by using existing images. In a project involving an infill site, for example, photographs of the existing context can be taken, traced over, and used as base drawings to design and present the new scheme in context. Existing vanishing points can be established and details of the design worked into the perspective view with varying degrees of accuracy, depending upon the level of completion reached. The tracing of perspective views is often undertaken by using translucent paper over an opaque image, or by the use of a light table to facilitate clarity. Slides of the intended context (which may also be taken of a model of the surrounding buildings built as a design tool and subsequently used as a generator of perspective images) may also be projected onto an opaque surface and traced, giving the designer the ability to choose the size of the final graphic image.

Figure 3.23
This perspective view of a scheme for Boston's North Square was developed by sketching over and altering a projected photographic image.

SPATIAL EXPLORATION AND THE COMPUTER

Many designers have come to value the flexibility of the computer in developing almost limitless perspective views of existing or designed space and form. Depending on the quality of programs and the hardware available, it is possible to create images in most of the conventional drawing types and to investigate their spatial characteristics from a variety of viewpoints. Similar generation of hand-drawn images would take considerably longer. Particularly useful is the generation of images that enable the designer to explore space in a sequential order, as if walking through the design. Similarly, images can be constructed from aerial viewpoints and even programmed to show how the sun will fall onto a structure at a given time of the day, month, and year, a particularly useful technique in designing energy-conscious buildings.

Computer-generated graphics do not typically create "realistic" drawings, but show all major construction lines, rather like an X ray. This may not be a problem for skilled computer users or designers, who may even value the information given by the skeletal images in helping them understand the qualities of the forms and spaces depicted. However, viewers unfa-

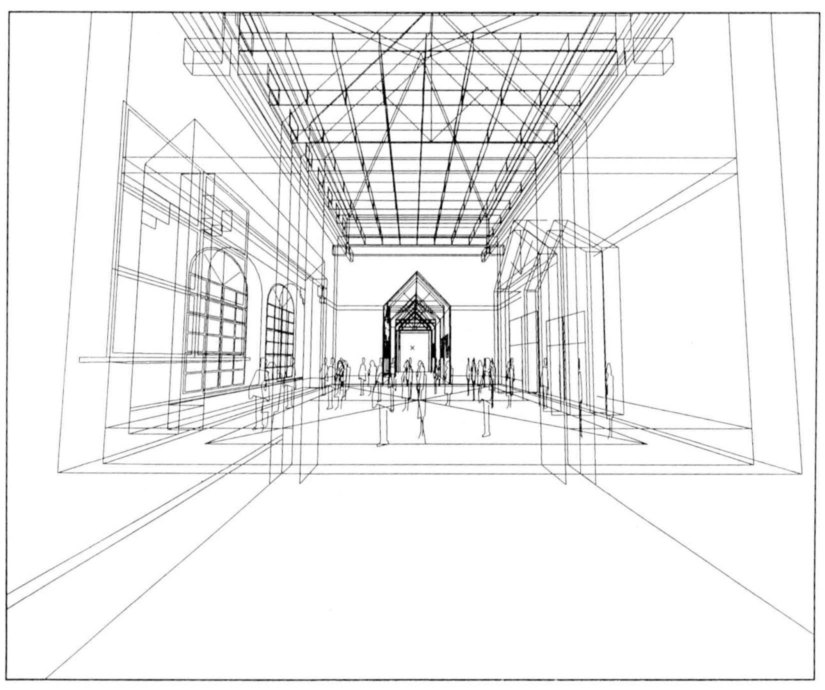

Figures 3.24–3.26
Perspectives generated by computer-aided design facilities can provide numerous skeletal images from a range of viewpoints.

miliar with computer drawings may experience great difficulty in reading the more complex "transparent" configurations. The presentor may therefore wish to improve the clarity of the images by erasing some of the hidden lines, cutting and repasting the drawings, or even tracing the most relevant information onto another surface by hand. With more sophisticated systems, a hidden-line algorithm may be incorporated into the process to eliminate nonessential lines and make viewing much easier.

Computer-generated work may present some problems not only in client comprehension but also in the desired quality of the final image. Most basic systems will be limited in their speed of image generation and the size and quality of the printout. Some designers cut and paste printouts into larger and more polished presentation formats, or even redraw images in a personal, freehand style. More sophisticated equipment gives the designer greater flexibility in the quality and content of the final product, permitting their presentation onto high-resolution paper or even onto a video cassette recorder or electric slide maker for less conventional presentations.

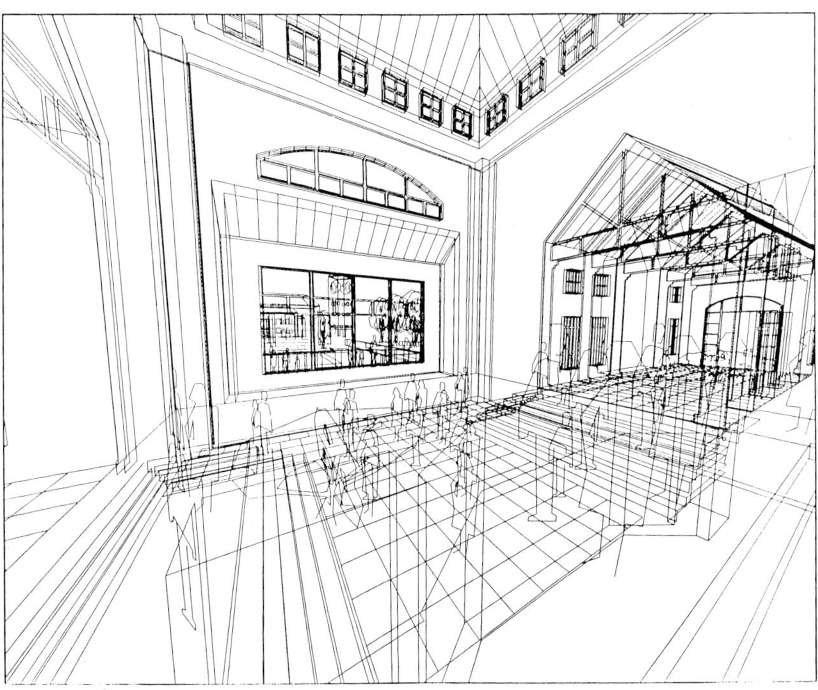

PICTORIAL REALISM AND THE METAPHOR

The depiction of an architectural design in a realistic setting with sky, trees, figures, and complete entourage is a familiar tradition in many architectural drawings. Before 1750, however, such drawings were rarely produced. Among the first architects to make use of pictorial realism was Sir William Chambers, who was influenced by the works of Piranesi and perhaps by Italian stage set design. An example of his work was a mausoleum, which was conveyed not as an ideal geometric form or in working-drawing format but as an atmospheric impression showing how the building might actually appear after years of use and weathering. Mature vegetation, rain- and soot-weathered stone, and crumbling, ruinous masonry were used to depict a new design, rather than provide a record of an existing building. With these techniques, Chambers was able to instill his design with a sense of timelessness and elevate the work to that of the ruins of classical antiquity. Pictorial realism was thus used as a communicative device which could provide drawings with symbolic and metaphorical content.

Mood, character, intent, and referential symbols can all be contained in pictorial rendering. Le Corbusier, for example, often made use of the symbolic potential of pictorial realism, even including a sketch of a picturesque painting by the painter Chatelet in the background of one of his perspective design sketches. With a simple arrangement of tree, rock, and temple, Le Corbusier was able to recall a ruinous, romantic landscape and all of its associative values—picturesque theory, rustic idylls, and the ruins of Classicism. By contrast, the airplanes and automobiles which filled Le Corbusier's urban design drawings of the 1920s contained the imagery of industry, speed, and the "brave new world" which served to intensify his theoretical stance. Le Corbusier also made use of everyday association: a table set for dinner, a half-full glass, or an open book can be found in his drawings, lending a sense of domestic (or, in some cases, monastic) reality. This technique allowed the viewer to imagine that everyday life was represented in these interiors, which, if drawn differently, might appear harsh and inaccessible. By making the viewer associate with the scene, the drawings have the capacity to assert themselves as "real" and buildable.

Typically, architects make little use of the symbolic possibilities of pictorial realism, employing it instead to make drawings readable by clients and nonarchitects. However, the addition of figures, cars, trees, and similar elements is useful in providing scale and a sense of reality to the most basic drawings and can be easily transposed into the design process by the use of basic tracing techniques or by computer generation.

Figure 3.27
This perspective drawing depicts a scheme for Milwaukee's lakefront, featuring a series of romantic off-shore islands. Entourage elements photocopied from the folios of Schinkel were used to make certain symbolic references to early nineteenth-century romanticism.

Section Two

GRAPHIC TECHNIQUES

Chapter Four
Color Application

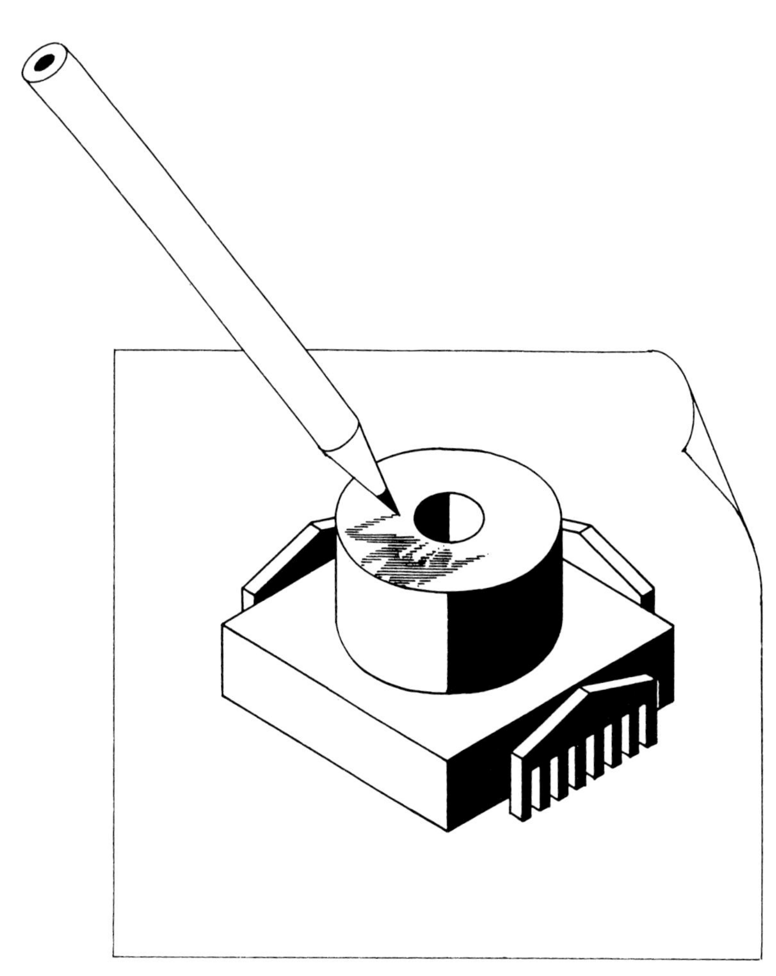

The introduction of color into design work provides a new dimension to the communication of ideas and gives the designer an added flexibility in their generation. Color techniques can be used to differentiate or code elements of a design or to provide a degree of realism or "atmosphere" to images. However, despite the added dimensions that can be introduced, it is interesting to see how the relationship between drawing and color has changed over the last few hundred years. In the eighteenth and nineteenth centuries, for example, watercolor and ink washes were frequently used not solely in the presentation of ideas but also in the design process. Two 1985 exhibitions in Chicago and London from the Royal Institute of British Architects archives collection demonstrated the widespread use of color media in architectural drawing throughout the design process during those centuries. However, exhibits from the first half of the twentieth century tended to be largely monochromatic, reflecting the general abandonment of color by the profession in favor of ink or pencil. This may in part flow from the ideological consequences of the Modern Movement, which, as has been previously argued, led to changes in delineation types and the rise in prominence of the paraline. However, the need for reproducibility of drawings in a construction industry of growing complexity also led to the reduction in use of colored drawings, which by their nature were not suited to multiple copying. Thus, the medium which was most appropriate to the process of reproducibility, black line on transparent paper, became the predominant means of drawing and therefore of generating and presenting design ideas.

That this move away from colored drawings has affected the final appearance of the buildings they depict is an intriguing and by no means original argument, and it is not the purpose of this chapter to explore it further. However, the relationship between drawing and form and the move toward monochromaticity is perhaps best expressed by Reyner Banham in his description of Paul Rudolph's Arts and Architecture Building at Yale:

> It is one of the very few buildings I know which, when photographed, was exactly like a drawing, with all the shading on the outside coming out as if it were ruled in with a very soft pencil . . . So that it is a building for draftsmanship and a building conceived *in terms* of draftsmanship.
> From S. Abercrombie, *AIA Journal* (book review), September 1982, p. 68.

Beyond any impacts upon the environment, an obvious consequence of a diminution in the use of color is the loss of associated understanding involved in its application. A number of valuable techniques which were once regularly employed by designers have been to a large extent neglected, and only in the past few years with the resurgence of interest in historicism has color again started to become a prime component in design drawings. Works by leading architects such as Michael Graves and James Stirling are published widely and have resulted in a new interest in colored media, especially colored pencils, pastels, and watercolor. This chapter, therefore, will explore the use of color in relation to the design and presentation processes and will investigate the specific applicability of the three media just mentioned.

UNDERSTANDING COLOR

Many architects regard the use of color as a final application to a completed design; others see its advantages if introduced in the formative design stages. In either case, it is important for the designer to have a basic understanding of color application. This involves knowledge of the media which may be used, their technical properties, and their means of application. Also, and perhaps most importantly, designers need to understand the appropriateness of the use of color both in various stages of the design process and in various types of projects. Although a detailed understanding of these matters is desirable, a rudimentary introduction can help to eliminate a number of problems, so the following sections provide a general account of the types and use of color.

SELECTING COLOR

An understanding of basic color theory enables the designer to select appropriate combinations of colors for specific projects. Knowing the components of hue, value, and chroma can ensure that colors selected will achieve the correct balance of contrast or complement and that the final graphic effect sought can be achieved. However, in the absence of a scientific knowledge of color properties, the media can be either underutilized or inappropriately applied. It is not uncommon, for example, for inexperienced designers confronted with a wide choice of colors in a medium to indiscriminately apply them without regard for their cumulative impact. The results often are garish and sometimes even detract from the graphic image. In the absence of a foundation of color theory, some simple experimentation can reduce the risk of poor application. Careful selection of a range of colors, preferably all with the same chromatic value (that is, the same "greyness" saturation), gives a greater chance of color coordination. The color hues should be selected on the basis of their compatibility or contrast and should be limited to a small number. The designer should then experiment briefly with the colors to establish the various combinations, mixes, and effects that are possible. A narrow range of colors and some experimentation, particularly prior to working on presentation-quality drawings, are essential for designers inexperienced in the use of color.

COLOR APPLICATION

The introduction of color into the designer's work provides an added dimension that can be used for information, clarification, or impression. However, the use of color in a graphic image may vary in its proximity to reality, and its effect should be considered before application. Color may be representative or may convey a sense of realism.

REPRESENTATIVE COLOR

Color may be applied in a way that does not convey a sense of real space or form but provides a more abstract level of information for the viewer. This color may be symbolic or atmospheric.

Symbolic Color

Various colors can be used in graphic images to represent abstractions and to act as clarifying codes, conveying information to the viewer that a monochromatic image could not. For example, different colors may be used to convey different functions or zones on maps or drawings depicting various materials.

These codes may have traditional associations which will be understood by an audience—for example, green for grass or blue for sky. Similarly, certain color conventions are attached to building elements and functions, such as blue and red to indicate cold and hot waterpipes. However, if the use of color has any representative value beyond simple differentiation of spaces or visual clarity and its purpose is not immediately apparent, an explanatory key should be provided somewhere on the drawing.

"Atmospheric" Color

Color can be applied purely to create an effect or impart "flavor" to a piece of graphic work. As with symbolic color, the palette can be chosen on a basis other than representative realism. The intent is to create an impressionistic vision of a scheme, conveying a sense of place or general atmosphere by giving a quick, imprecise vision which simplifies details in order to capture the basic essence of a design. Thus, the application draws on artistic rather than architectural standards, and the choice of color type and mix may require considerable research and experimentation before any finished work is attempted.

REALISTIC COLOR

Where color is added to an image in order to create the illusion of reality, the palette should be selected on the basis of how realistically the medium represents actual materials, surfaces, or elements in the environment. This is perhaps the most difficult application to successfully achieve, as accurately matching the color of, for example, brickwork with the raw color of pencil or paint requires much skill and practice. The problem is compounded by issues of scale. As most images are drawn at a fraction of the original size, the color and texture being depicted must, according to the principles of atmospheric perspective, be reduced accordingly. Mastering the art of color accuracy *and* reduction may require a great deal of practice and experimentation before a satisfactory image is produced. The impact of realistic images can be great, however, and they can be effective and persuasive in presentations to clients and audiences.

COLORED PENCILS

Colored pencils, like all media, possess distinct characteristics and limitations which make some graphic effects relatively easy to achieve, others extremely difficult. Working in pencil may encourage the designer to draw those effects which are most easily achieved, which may affect the design itself. It is important therefore to understand the significance of colored pencil application in both design and presentation.

The basic characteristic of drawing with colored pencil is the use of the line, which can be generated as easily as by ordinary pencil. Achieving large areas of flat, even color is a more difficult process, accomplished only by building up accumulations of numerous lines, which can be a time-consuming and sometimes ineffective technique. These characteristics are completely different than, for example, those of watercolor, by which large areas of color can be applied quickly and effectively, although fine-line detail is often more problematic. In practice, the line quality of the colored pencil is more appropriate to some applications than others, and it may deflect the designer's attention from important design considerations in favor of ones that are easier to draw. For example, windows are often shown with rendered mullions, which are easily drawn with single strokes of the pencil, while the window pane is either left uncolored or lightly shaded. Although fast to complete, the rendering does not represent the actual appearance of the window, where the panes will typically be the darkest element of the facade. The same misapplication in other design situations, where an inappropriate medium is used in a way that distorts the designer's perception or implicit intent, should be avoided wherever possible. All media should be used solely as tools, where their unique characteristics complement the individual design task.

If the limitations of colored pencils are understood, their use in appropriate situations can be very effective. Beyond the basic line, graphic effects can be achieved by mixing the colors into a composite "hatch," producing a complex, often vibrant, color that has more depth and complexity than a straight application of a single color. This technique derives to some degree from the theories of such French colorists as Picasso, Delacroix, and Seurat, the last of whom experimented with subtle tones and hues in his paintings. Colored pencil mixing has distinct differences from other architectural media, particularly watercolor and pastel, where premixing produces a flat, even tone composed of the color ingredients. Colored pencil mixing offers a coherently whole image, while at the same time showing individual color strokes which can enrich and enliven a drawing. Although this technique can sometimes mislead both the designer and intended audience as to the final appearance of a design, the composite application of colored pencil can produce some excellent representations of material, light, and shade that can greatly enhance the drawing.

PASTELS

Soft pastels, sometimes known as French pastels, are a type of high-quality chalk, usually manufactured in cylindrical or rectilinear stick form. While they are a somewhat unconventional architectural medium, they possess some unique characteristics which have great potential in both the design and presentation of architectural subjects.

Basically, pastel can quickly cover large areas of surface in a flat, even tone which would take considerably longer with colored pencil. The application of tone without resort to the line allows the depiction of mass with great ease and speed and can help to reduce the importance of planar edges in the composition of forms. As a presentation tool, too, pastels are invaluable in rapidly laying down flat, even washes of tone to highlight or accentuate design drawings.

Although similar in some respects to watercolor, pastel retains all the advantages of a dry medium. It can be reworked, erased, or added to without any delays in drying, and it can be used on thin, unprepared surfaces such as trace or print paper which would normally warp badly if a wet color were applied.

Erasure Drawing

Although it is feasible to use pastels in the same additive way as other colored media, it is also possible to experiment with an entirely different technique which is essentially the reverse of traditional drawing. In erasure drawing, a surface is covered with areas of dark pastel color, often formed by mixing several colors together. Details and forms are then highlighted by erasing pigment in a way that describes the play of light and shadows on the intended forms.

In this way, the designer is directly sketching light and its effects on mass rather than following the conventional method of using dark pencils to draw in shadows. Not only is the technique fast and effective, it can help the designer to address the question of light and shade in design, which may often be seen as secondary in importance to the built form itself.

The messy, imprecise nature of pastels may dissuade some architects from introducing them into a process which they may feel requires crispness and accuracy. However, there is no reason why they cannot be used to supplement line drawings with fast "washes" of color in a manner reminiscent of the traditional pen-and-ink wash. If the unconventional nature of pastel as a design tool can be accepted, it can prove to be an extraordinarily flexible addition to traditional media, providing some invaluable techniques for the understanding and depiction of space and form.

WATERCOLOR

Watercolor and ink washes have traditionally been used as basic architectural techniques in both design and presentation. The Royal Institute of British Architects archives contains numerous examples of renderings, which vary from notebook sketches to exquisitely detailed designs by architects such as Lutyens, Chambers, and Voysey. However, despite its long history, watercolor has fallen into disuse during the era of the Modern Movement, and the techniques of application have been largely neglected. This is unfortunate, as the unique qualities of watercolor can provide remarkable visual effects if used correctly.

Although similar to pastel in the rapid application of an even wash onto a large surface area, watercolor is essentially a translucent medium, allowing the quality of the surface and any marks made on it to show through. Thus, it can be used to produce delicate, almost ethereal images in sketch form or, by the cumulative addition of "sheets" of the color, to create a composite image forming a lively, atmospheric drawing.

If used in opaque form, watercolor takes on an entirely different character and is closer in effect to oil or acrylic paints. The essence of its use in architectural rendering lies in the translucency of the paint when applied in a highly diluted form. The result is necessarily a subtle one, and if a more powerful graphic impact is required, another medium should be selected. The translucency of the finish also requires that the surface be of reasonable quality, as any imperfections or marks will be seen through most washes. However, there is no reason why colored pencil, graphite pencil, or ink cannot be added to or used in conjunction with the technique to embellish the quality of the sheet.

The basic technique of successful watercolor application lies in very simple principles involving adequately diluted color applied evenly and regularly onto a tilted surface. Once this has been mastered by limited experimentation, composite washes are easy to achieve both quickly and effectively. More complex effects can be introduced by, for example, adding color to saturated sheets to form random, atmospheric patterns, although these techniques tend to move away from basic architectural applications.

Figure 4.1 (at left)
Chalk-type pastels were used to illustrate various levels, including water, lower and upper terrace levels, and pavilions. Principles of color application, derived from the Beaux-Arts conventions of recession and advancement, are used symbolically with little attempt at pictorial realism.

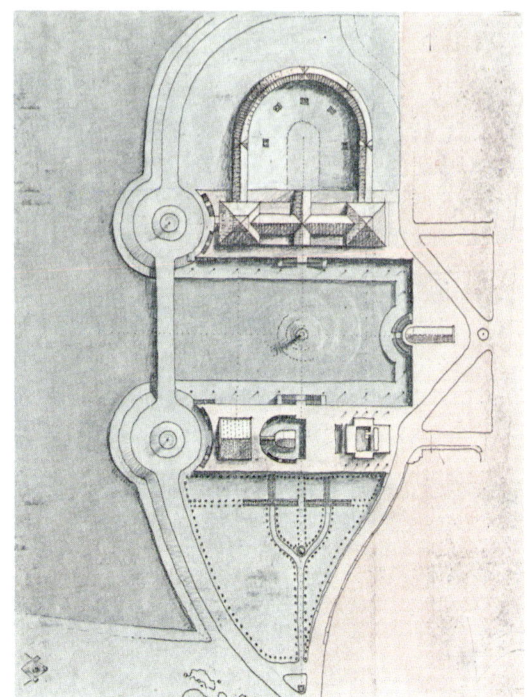

Figure 4.2 (at right)
The colors and deep tones of an impending storm give this drawing a powerful, atmospheric quality. The drawing depicts a liberty monument for San Francisco Bay and was executed in colored pencil over a color photograph of a clay model.

Figure 4.3
Moonlit clouds, shaded foliage, and rich colors attempt to bestow this drawing with an atmosphere of romanticism and the mood of an evening in August. Although the drawing is romantic in mood, materials and textures are treated realistically. See Figure 3.13 for comparison.

Figure 4.4
Colored pencils were used to develop this "realistic" sketch of streetscape treatment for a village in Wisconsin.

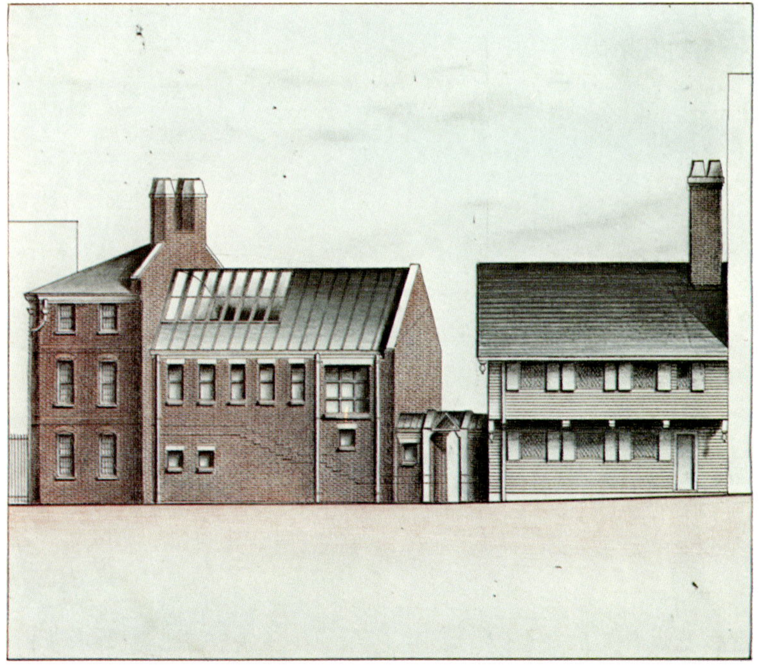

Figure 4.5
Brick texture was photographically reduced to the proper scale and then cut and pasted into an ink line drawing. A pastel sky, brick color, and colored pencil details were added to produce this realistic elevation.

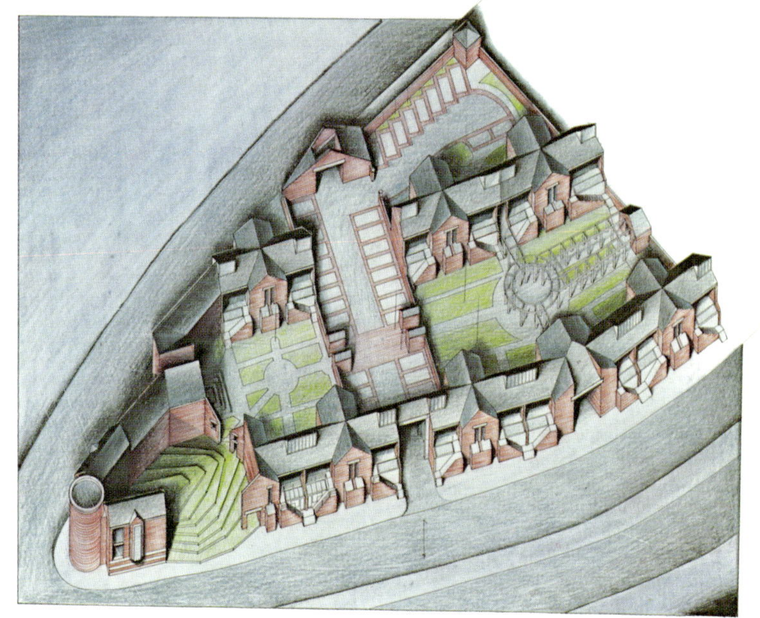

Figure 4.6
Pastels and colored pencils were used to color this ink line drawing of a housing project. Heavy shadows help the drawing to read three dimensionally. Compare with Figure 2.13.

Figure 4.7
Deep shadows and intense colors were used to describe the quality of a late summer afternoon in the courtyard. Foreground shadows help to articulate elements behind the viewer, which are then clarified in the plan view above. The deep tones also lend a somewhat sinister or tragic quality to the view. Compare with Figure 3.11.

Figure 4.8
This drawing of a visionary interior was achieved by entirely covering an ink line drawing with pastel and then using an electric eraser to etch areas of light tone.

Figure 4.9
Simple watercolor techniques involving the application of fine, translucent films of color can be effective in building up images. Contrast and shading are emphasized by adding more coats of color or by accentuating edges with colored or lead pencil.

Chapter Five
Collage Techniques

Techniques of collage are usually associated with fine arts and other related disciplines, but they can be useful in more architecturally related activities in both the design and presentation processes. In its most basic form, collage involves the manipulation of two-dimensional surfaces into various patterns or relationships. The relative shape and area of the piece of paper or card used in this exercise can relate to simple geometric shapes, colors, or textures or can be used in a representative way to depict spaces, elements, or functions. The technique provides a speed of manipulation and immediacy of results not readily available in more conventional methods of delineation and can help to simplify design issues to a point where they can be easily manipulated.

Collage has certain limitations which should be considered when it is used. Primarily, the inflexibility of the prepared pieces may tend to limit the designer's attention to the potential variety that may otherwise be generated with more fluid techniques. The acceptance of certain fixed shapes, which may carry implications of room shape and size, may be restrictive and cause the designer to concentrate on the relationships between these shapes rather than the functions they seek to represent. Furthermore, the exercise of moving objects around tends to reduce the importance of surrounding space, which, if not carefully handled, can become residual. As collage is primarily two-dimensional, space is difficult to design simultaneously in plan, elevation, and section. However, the technique, although perhaps the least used in the conventional design process, has some useful applications, particularly if used in conjunction with other drawing types. This chapter, therefore, illustrates the application of collage techniques in both the design and presentation processes and outlines some broad methodologies for their effective implementation.

COLLAGE IN THE DESIGN PROCESS

When Josef Abers was the head of fine arts instruction at Yale, he introduced his classes to a series of exercises involving Coloraid paper in a variety of colors and shapes. The students manipulated these to form organizations and patterns in order to expand their understanding of spatial interactions of form. The same basic technique can be transferred to building design in both plan and elevational development.

Collage in Plan

At the beginning of each design project, the designer must transfer spatial requirements into a visual format so that the relative size and relationships of the spaces can be seen in a comprehensive layout. This may present some difficulties, particularly to the inexperienced designer, who may have had little practice in manipulating spaces quickly and to scale. Sketches are usually used to convey the approximate proportions of the spaces involved, and a series of overlaid diagrams, perhaps worked over gridded paper to provide a degree of uniformity and scale, can be useful in exploring design alternatives. This technique, however, can be partially replaced or enhanced by the use of collage techniques. If room area sizes are known or can be approximated, they can be drawn onto card or paper and cut out. If only square footage is known and space proportions are as yet undetermined, a number of alternative shapes generated from the same area can be prepared to give the designer more flexibility in their arrangement.

When all the shapes representing spaces are prepared, they can be manipulated into various configurations. In this way, the designer can quickly become familiar with the relative sizes of the project, as well as developing an understanding of the potential layouts that may be possible. The technique is intended only as an introductory step at the basic design level. Once the designer has determined a preference within the alternatives suggested by the collage work, the solutions that seem to be the most appropriate can be regenerated in a drawn medium. In some cases, particular configurations of the shapes can be recorded simply by quickly drawing around their perimeters, leaving a record which can be worked over with tracing paper at a later stage. Care should be taken when using this approach, however, not to become too reliant on the collage elements as the sole generators of design. Too much concentration on the plan and a tendency to piece the cut-outs together in a way that creates an irregular footprint (which may be difficult to make compatible with a three-dimensional building) is undesirable, and a suitable balance between collage, drawings, and even models should be sought.

Collage techniques have their most obvious application in the layout of buildings, although there is no reason why they cannot be used to organize spaces other than interior rooms and incorporate external areas related to building, such as gardens, paths, and drives. In the scheme illustrated, elements of the design—building, car park, gardens, terraces—were stylized into shapes in approximate proportion to sizes dictated by site constraints and project requirements. These were then cut out from a variety of colored papers and manipulated into various configurations. The more successful of these exercises were then used to generate design drawings which reintroduced the realistic constraints of the project—such as vehicular access and specific rooms and activities—but which kept within the broad conceptual framework of the scheme generated by the collage layouts. The final design indicates a powerful overall image which derived largely from the freedom of the designer to concentrate on the broader issues instead of too many physical restraints by using the stylized collage elements.

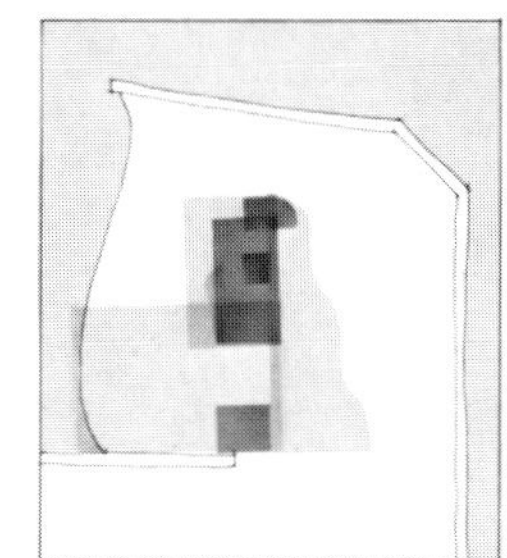
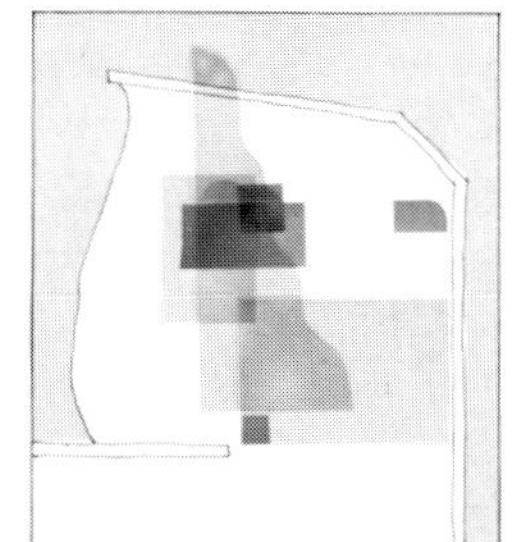
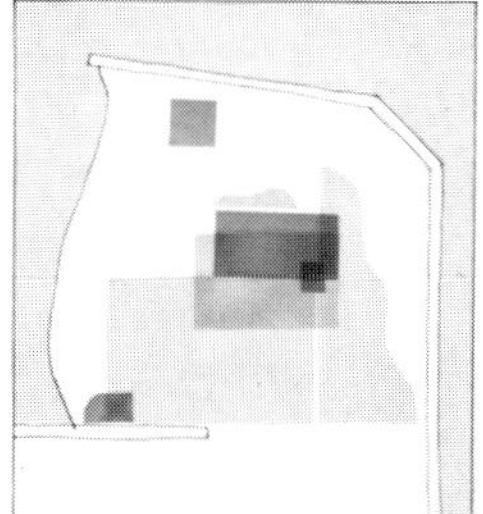

Figure 5.1 (at left)
The four alternative layouts pieced together from the selected collage elements indicate the potential configurations available on the site.

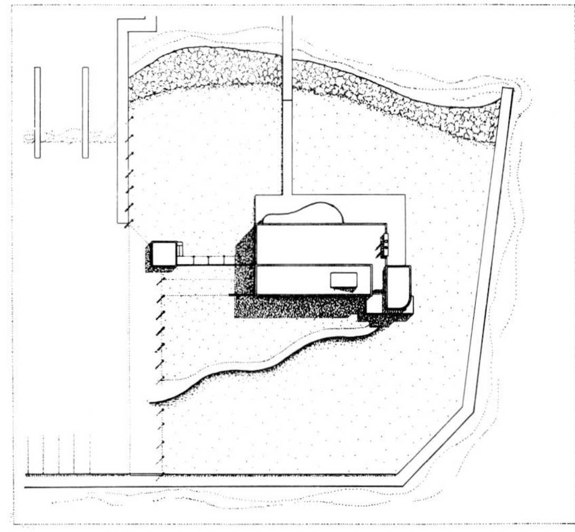

Figure 5.2 (at right)
The design of the building and site has been finalized, and detail and accurate scale have been added to the parti generated by the collage elements.

Urban Design and Collage

Collage techniques may also be effectively employed in urban scaled designs. By reconstructing existing building footprints in collage, the interrelationships of the elements and the overall nature of the city fabric can be studied clearly. In addition, a number of proposed building figure ground shapes can be generated to complete or complement the existing urban spatial patterns. However, several alternatives should be produced so that more detailed design strategies are not inhibited by fixed footprints. This technique allows the designer the advantages of perceiving the overall site context is a way that may not be afforded by simple reference to a site map, and it addresses the criticism often aimed at contemporary architects that they tend to concentrate on the building form as an object, treating the surrounding spaces as a residual, secondary concern.

An extension to this technique has been developed to enable the integration of collage into the design process at a more detailed level. Instead of using simple figure ground shapes to depict building plans within an existing context, previously drawn articulated building plans and landscape elements such as pergolas or formal gardens can be redrawn or printed from maps or drawings and used as collage cutouts in the design process. The process of arrangement is fast and flexible, enabling the designer to concentrate on the broader spatial issues rather than on the more specific design of elements. With relatively little effort, a great number of alternatives can be generated, which, owing to the defined nature of the collage cutouts, show a great deal about the design implications of each scheme. This technique is particularly adaptable to housing design, where prototypical unit plans can be collected, copied, and used as principal elements in a collage study.

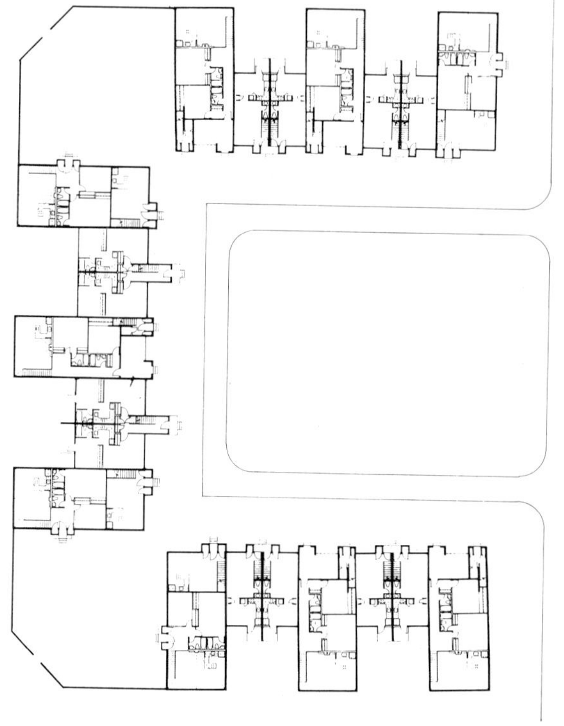

Figure 5.3
Several housing units were designed and drawn to a 1″ = 8′ scale. These images were then reduced, copied, and configured to create a collage of a small square. Once the images were pasted down, only a few lines had to be added to complete the drawing.

Collage in Elevation

Collage techniques may be equally effective in designing elevations, both on a single building or in a composite setting such as a street or city square. Inexperienced designers may have difficulty in composing facades which adequately incorporate the surface with its openings and any applied building elements (downspouts, porches, etc.). Inadequate attention to proportion, hierarchy, and balance in the design process can often lead to an unattractive or inappropriate appearance of the facade.

The ability of collage to separate and simplify elements of a design helps to free the designer's mind of the complexity of the relationships and allows greater flexibility in their manipulation. For example, a variety of simple massing shapes depicting the building facade can be produced, supplemented with a variety of window and door shapes, porches, gutters, downspouts, lintels, and even roofing configurations. The simplicity of the elements, especially if they are cut from different shades of card, allows the designer to concentrate on developing compatible arrangements of shapes into a coherent whole. Based upon these exercises, the best results can be transferred to a drawing medium, where detail and refinement can be added.

Figure 5.4
The church in this view of North Square, Boston, was assembled by collaging pieces of photocopied texture, windows, and drawn detail in an attempt to reconstruct the appearance of the church, which was demolished in 1775–6. The church was then pasted into the site to re-create an early nineteenth-century view of North Square.

Subtractive Collage

The approach described above relies largely on the additive nature of the elements, where the designer compounds the design by adding and overlapping the collage shapes depicting building elements. A variation to the procedure, and one which may provide a different perspective to the elevational treatment, takes a subtractive approach. Instead of adding elements to the base facade shape, the designer can instead cut out intended openings or setbacks. This approach would be most suited to building types where the intent of the designer is to maintain the concept of a formal element (a cube, for example) but etch out or erode some parts without eliminating the basic shape.

Contextual Collage

When designing within the context of an existing street or similar assembly of buildings, the same techniques can be used. Collage may be employed as an analytical tool to study the surroundings in terms of their shape, window/wall relationships, and detail and to help the designer understand the nature of the area before attempting to add to it. Similarly, the technique can be used in elevational design, taking elements from the existing context and introducing them into the new scheme. Although care should be taken not to produce copies or parodies of the surrounding buildings, the abstract nature of the collage shapes gives the designer ample latitude in reinterpreting the final detailed design into a contemporary solution.

Figure 5.5
Brick texture, photographically reduced to the proper scale, was cut and pasted into an ink line drawing. The texture of dark bricks and light mortar joints helps to convey an accurate sense of the size and scale of the building.

COLLAGE IN THE PRESENTATION PROCESS

The speed and effectiveness of image generation in the design process using collage techniques can be carried over into the presentation of ideas. As appearance now becomes an important factor, however, the kinds of surface utilized should be chosen with care, and their individual properties used accordingly.

Papers are the most useful, as they are easy to cut and can be layered without becoming bulky. The variety of textures, colors, and thicknesses also give them a wide application. Thicker paper and cards may also be effective in presentation, particularly in providing depth cues. By virtue of their thickness, collage elements can overlap other elements on the composition, giving prominence, for example, to a building facade and giving a sense of perspective to the image. Similarly, windows or recesses can be cut from elevations to show their relative depth and provide a shadow line within the cutouts. The effectiveness of this technique will depend upon the thickness of the material and the skill of the presenter, and some experimentation may be necessary to ensure an acceptable result.

The application of translucent surfaces may also be regarded as a collage technique. This usually involves specially manufactured adhesive sheets of color or shading which can be applied to artwork, providing a uniform, professional finish which will reproduce well. The machinelike quality of the final graphic, which can be achieved in a wide range of monochromatic or colored alternatives, can be very effective in a presentation format, although care should be taken to match the technique to appropriate design schemes.

Another technique which can be used in conjunction with translucent surfaces (tracing paper, mylar, and vellum) involves the use of a collage sheet which is applied to the back of the image, thus highlighting a particular zone of the drawing. Usually, white backing sheets will read the most powerfully through the translucent sheet, although colored papers may be used to produce a muted, tonal effect.

Collage techniques can also be introduced into the presentation process if they are used to generate finished images of the final design, where their speed and visual impact can be very effective. For example, powerful, comprehensive graphic compositions can be assembled very quickly by introducing collage elements which represent sky, trees, or building lines behind an elevation, or floor and ground surfaces in plan. Color and texture can also be considered in the choice of collage materials to provide another level of detail and graphic impact. In more detailed drawings, the collage elements may be cut from sheets which are printed with a recognizable texture, such as brickwork or groundcover, and applied to areas of the graphic image. This technique, if used carefully, can provide a sense of detail and completion which would be both slow and difficult to achieve using conventional drawing methods. Similarly, additional entourage elements such as skies, cars, trees, and people can be photocopied and applied to drawings for atmospheric or contextual effect. Again, if used carefully and appropriately, the extra information can provide a convincing degree of sophistication to a drawing at a cost of very little time or effort.

Figures 5.6–5.7
Compare before and after views of an ink line drawing which was collaged with sky and foliage. Photocopied from an eighteenth-century etching.

REPROGRAPHIC TECHNIQUES

Although many collage applications require only blank surfaces, some of the more sophisticated techniques previously described may require the replication of existing artwork. Relatively recent technological advances in this field have made an entire range of reprographic alternatives available to designers, which can provide speed of application and effectiveness of impact if used appropriately.

In the past, the basic replication techniques commonly available to designers were largely limited to paper-to-paper or trace-to-paper transfers. These utilized either wet or dry processes, and both were usually printed onto thin paper with varying degrees of quality. Contemporary machinery has improved the quality of copying enormously and has provided greater flexibility in the type of copy available. Not only can duplicates be made in a wide range of colors and tones, but the surfaces onto which an image is reproduced can vary from a translucent film to a thick paper or card capable of carrying graphic applications such as watercolor. These alternatives are further enhanced by the capacity to accurately reproduce even the subtlest color rendering without recourse to traditional photographic methods.

The ability to reduce and enlarge images is now a facility common to many copy machines and has greatly enhanced the designer's ability to utilize existing images by matching their scale to the project at hand. Similarly, the designer's own work, when complete, can be effectively reproduced at any scale so that full-scale presentations can be reduced to a size suitable for mailing, storage, or even presentation in a report-sized format.

The availability of sophisticated technology in reprographics has provided the designer with an invaluable tool, enabling fast, quality printing at a variety of sizes and onto a range of surfaces. One must, however, explore its full potential to avoid underutilization. Two imaginative collage techniques have recently been developed which illustrate ways of expanding the use of copying devices beyond basic reproduction. In the first, the light–dark control of the printer is adjusted while several copies are taken of the same image so that each is a different shade. These images are then cut and pasted together so that a composite image is assembled using the different tones. In this way, the final picture derives a sense of hierarchy from the chosen quality of darkness or lightness given to, for example, walls, floors, and furniture, but has a consistency of appearance derived from the paper quality and printing process.

In the second technique, whole images can be assembled by bringing together entourage elements culled from a variety of sources and in a range of scaled sizes. Imaginative ideas can be generated with remarkably little time and effort, providing high-quality final images that can be used to provide the impetus for further design work.

Figure 5.8
A very quick and simple sketch is transformed by collaging it onto an eighteenth-century etching of a sky and embellishing the image with script press-type.

Figure 5.9
This poster illustration was produced by collaging at least ten distinct views, photographs, elevations, and etchings into a single fantasy image of New York. Film tone and additional drawing help to fuse the collaged pieces into a coherent illustration.

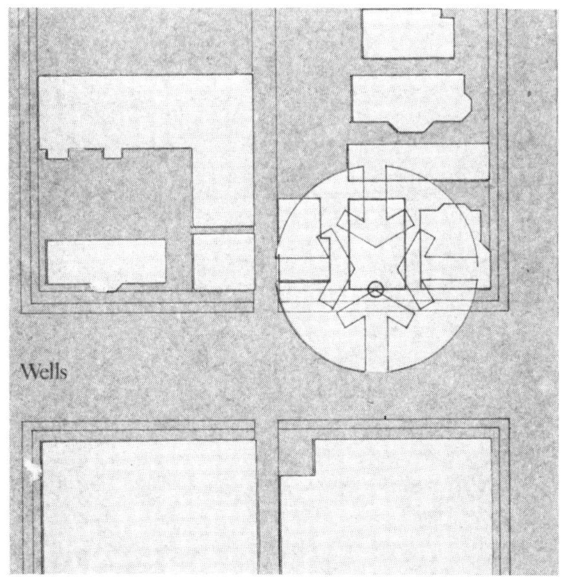

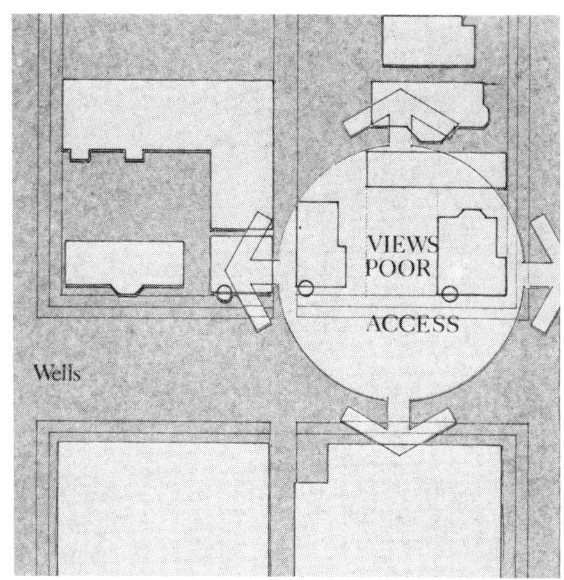

Figure 5.10
A line drawing was blueline printed at different printing speeds, producing images of light and dark tones. These were then collaged together into a single drawing containing distinct value contrast.

Figure 5.11
This fantasy landscape was produced by cutting and pasting a variety of photographs and drawings into a single perspective. Correction fluid and additional ink drawing were then added to help unify the images.

Chapter Six
Models

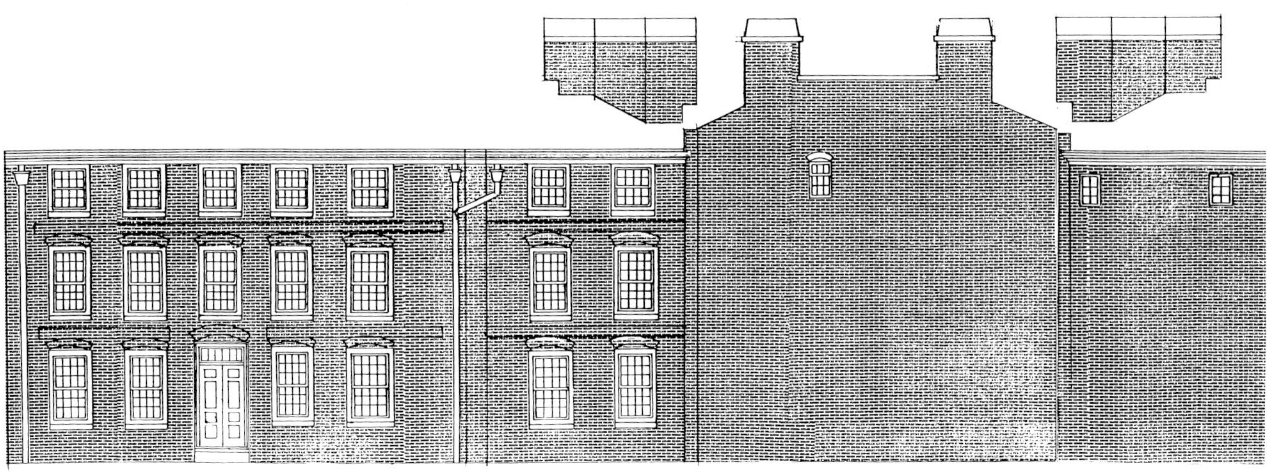

The use of three-dimensional models to represent space and form can be an effective means of exploring and communicating design ideas, serving as a useful alternative or supplement to basic drawing techniques. Model building lets the designer look at a design as a composite whole, as opposed to a number of separate parts (plan, elevation, etc.). It can then be evaluated from an almost infinite number of viewpoints, whereas perspective or axonometric renderings provide only one fixed view in each drawing. Even Alberti, who published the first treatise on perspective drawing, advised architects against using drawings to study three-dimensional form and suggested instead the use of models in conjunction with the plan view.

Models can be effective in exploring site issues, where the massing and spatial qualities of streets, neighborhoods, or even cities can be simplified and constructed at appropriate scales. Alternatively, building scale models enable the designer to visualize the external form of a proposed structure, while internal or breakaway models allow rooms to be seen as discrete figures within a form and can show spatial characteristics and relationships reasonably well.

If the model is simple in its construction, it can be readily changed to accommodate new design strategies. This can be more difficult with drawings, particularly constructed perspectives, which take a relatively long time to prepare, and may dissuade the designer from making changes entailing reconstruction of the drawings. In the presentation process, models can provide a representation of reality which may be easier for an audience or client to understand than conventional drawings.

However, it must be remembered that a model provides *only* a representation of reality. Issues of scale and detail are necessarily lost in the construction, which can be deceptive to both designers and audiences, who may assume that the final product will closely resemble the model form. The realistic nature of the model is also brought into question by the way in which it is usually viewed. The ability to explore spaces and forms from any number of angles must be tempered by the fact that few of the vantage points will ever be seen by the human eye. It is therefore possible to design a building which may look excellent from an aerial viewpoint but which in fact has ignored the perspective of the ground-level pedestrian. In addition, the construction of a study model as a singular object may be useful in focusing the designer's eye on the form of the intended building, but may tend to minimize the importance of the site and surrounding context and ignore the spatial issues of the design. This may not be a problem in a rural setting, although urban schemes where the building is conceived as an object may result in residual surrounding spaces.

Models offer a number of advantages in the design and presentation processes, although their limitations and the appropriateness of their application should be clearly understood. This chapter explores a variety of modeling types and their uses, in addition to their associated techniques of construction. It examines the appropriateness of models to particular situations, the techniques and materials necessary, and some shortcuts and pitfalls in their production.

MODELS OF OBJECTS VERSUS MODELS OF SPACE

Although models are usually conceived as solid, three-dimensional forms representing tangible objects such as buildings, they can be equally effective in the depiction of space, both in and between buildings. However, if the focus of the designer's mind is directed more towards the modeling of objects, spatial issues may become neglected. This neglect, it has often been claimed, is one of the causes of the poor quality of many urban areas, where inadequate attention to space has led to non-unified, chaotic, or simply nondescript residual areas. Spatial models utilized at the earlier stages of design may help to clarify the implications of designed space. Urban scale projects can benefit from the construction of a contextual siting model, which need not be particularly detailed but should be created at a scale which allows the designer to understand how additional forms will affect the existing spatial configurations.

More typically, models are used to represent building shapes and configurations, both at a schematic massing level and at a more detailed level, introducing such issues as visual appearance or constructional potential. However, overreliance on models as an accurate representation of reality can be a problem. The model of a building which can be rotated easily in the hands gives the creator an overall image of the form but can tend to minimize the importance of the ground-plane view. Consequences of this shortcoming may be reflected in highly designed roofing which, although visually strong from above, is virtually lost when viewed from normal eye height. Some designers, attempting to focus both their attention and that of an audience upon the realistic effects of a model, have constructed elaborate viewing procedures involving raised daises or limited-view apparatus. A simpler approach is the inclusion of perspective drawings to supplement the model, or the construction beneath it of a substantial ground plane, containing surrounding physical information such as trees, roads, and other buildings. This tends to remind observers of the content of the design and lessens the ''objectness'' of the model.

Massing Models

Models showing large-scale exterior space can be very flexible in their construction and can be useful in exploring the topographical features of a design, a particularly useful attribute on sloping or uneven sites. Simple angled or stacked configurations may enable the designer to grasp the qualities of the site, although where card or foam core is not sufficiently fluid, the designer may resort to clay to model the site's contours. Clay allows the designer to accurately sculpt the contours of the site and to change them easily with the addition of new design ideas. Similarly, clay may also be useful in molding simple building forms. The technique is fast and effective and, when used in conjunction with sketches and simple plans, can allow the designer to generate and refine design ideas through numerous iterations. Alternatively, rudimentary building forms can be constructed of chunks of wood, small piles of card, or even "found" objects, such as polystyrene blocks. As a learning tool, the model at this stage need not have a refined appearance, and speed of assembly and manipulation should determine the choice of media used in its construction.

Figure 6.1
This model of a housing project primarily shows the mass, omitting all detail such as windows, texture, and color. Built of card and clay, the model was then painted with brushed white acrylic, which conceals the quick, somewhat sloppy technique.

Models of Rooms

Simple modelmaking techniques can be used at a large scale to plan and determine the quality of interiors. Simple card partitions can quickly provide an indication of room size and shape, and the addition of rudimentary elements, possibly wooden blocks, can show furniture layout and equipment implications. More sophisticated versions of this kind of model can, by the incorporation of a roof and building openings, indicate the qualities of natural light which may be expected within the building, particularly if the model is used in conjunction with either a heliodon or artificial sky. This added dimension of knowledge, which can be obtained without recourse to complex calculations, makes the technique an invaluable one.

Figure 6.2
This model of an "outdoor room" depicts an urban park design for Boston. Photocopied brick texture was reduced to the proper scale and then spray-mounted onto thin card. Used in conjunction with painted balsa and twigs for trees, the model depicts only those elements which provide spatial enclosure for the "room."

Space as Solid and Space as Void

In order to gain a general appreciation of space, particularly at the larger-scale urban level, clay modeling may prove useful. For example, an existing or proposed site map can be covered with clay to the depth of approximately one inch, from which can be cut any squares, courtyards, or streets. The remaining clay configuration then gives the designer a comprehensive, if potentially abstract, vision of the relationship of urban spaces to the mass of building.

The use of clay in the design process can be taken one step further in helping to reveal spatial information. If architects have difficulty in envisioning space as a tangible quality, even the use of simulated forms may not be sufficient to provide adequate emphasis. An exercise which may help to focus attention on spatial quality still involves using clay modeling, but in a converse way. Instead of using the material to form tangible elements, a sizable chunk of clay can instead be regarded as solid space. From this, the imprints of buildings and other tangible elements can be carved. As the model is a simple one, a general impression of the shape will usually suffice. The resulting model will show the spatial implications of building configurations very powerfully by illustrating space as a solid, opaque form. This may help the designer to better understand how the space looks, and then to refine it accordingly with more accurate models and drawings.

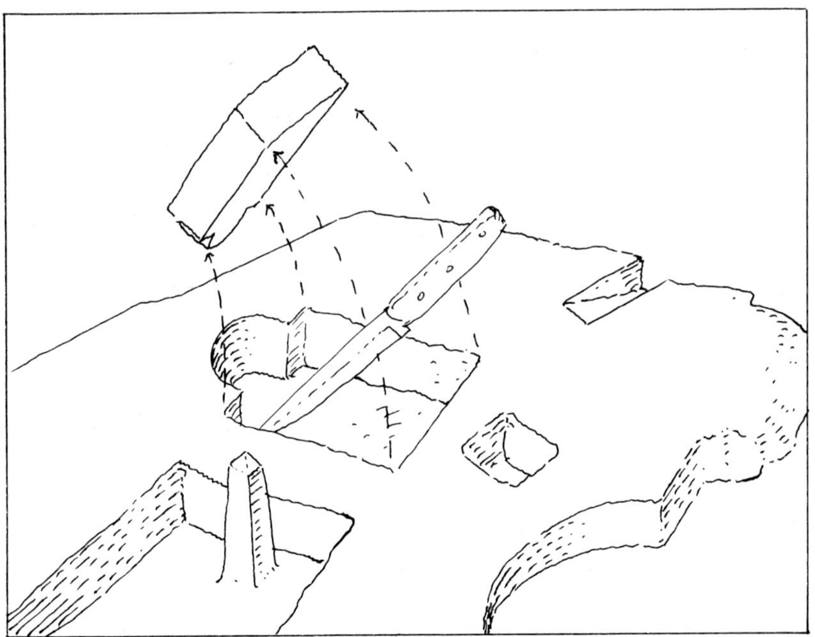

Figure 6.3
Models of "figural spaces" can be simply created by cutting voids from a lump of plasticine clay.

MODELS OF FACADES

It is possible, and in many cases desirable, to study a building's primary facade not as a drawing, but as a model. Rather than drafting elements such as windows and portals, they can be cut into or added onto a surface to provide a useful design tool.

This allows a designer to accurately judge the effects of such elements as projecting cornices, belt courses, and balconies by holding the study model in sunlight and observing the play of shadows. This technique works best with designs that are envisioned as "thick," modeled facades in which there are layers of space, or significant projections and recessions. The only drawback is that when an elevation is studied as a unique and singular element, it can be developed in isolation from the other aspects of a design. These models should therefore always be studied in conjunction with other drawing and model types.

There are certain situations in which facade models make ideal presentation tools, such as an infill design in a historic context, or when an elevation must be shown to laymen not familiar with drawing conventions. Such models are best displayed pinned to a wall as three-dimensional drawings.

Figure 6.4
The facade model records the existing condition of a group of buildings which are to be renovated.

SECTIONAL MODELS

Models can be built which describe a section cut through a building, allowing the designer or viewer to look into major interior spaces. Such models can reveal the relationships between exterior massing and interior volumes and can assist the designer in resolving problems of this type. Some sectional models are built in two parts which can be split apart to reveal interior views, while others depict only the section cut and part of the overall mass. These models can also communicate technical information by the addition to the section cut of drawn detail which describes aspects of the building's construction.

Figure 6.5
A sectional model of a residential interior.

COMPONENT MODELING

Designers will sometimes study individual building elements as models, usually in large-scale projects where models of the entire project show insufficient detail. A model of a single structural bay can be built, for example, to study the details and character of each element. This modeling technique is especially useful in designs where an element will be repeated, such as in a long colonnade or galleria, in which a single column may be used repeatedly. Rather than building a schematic model of the entire scheme, it may be preferable to build a highly detailed model of only a single section at a relatively large scale. As with all drawing and model types, component models should be developed in conjunction with other study methods.

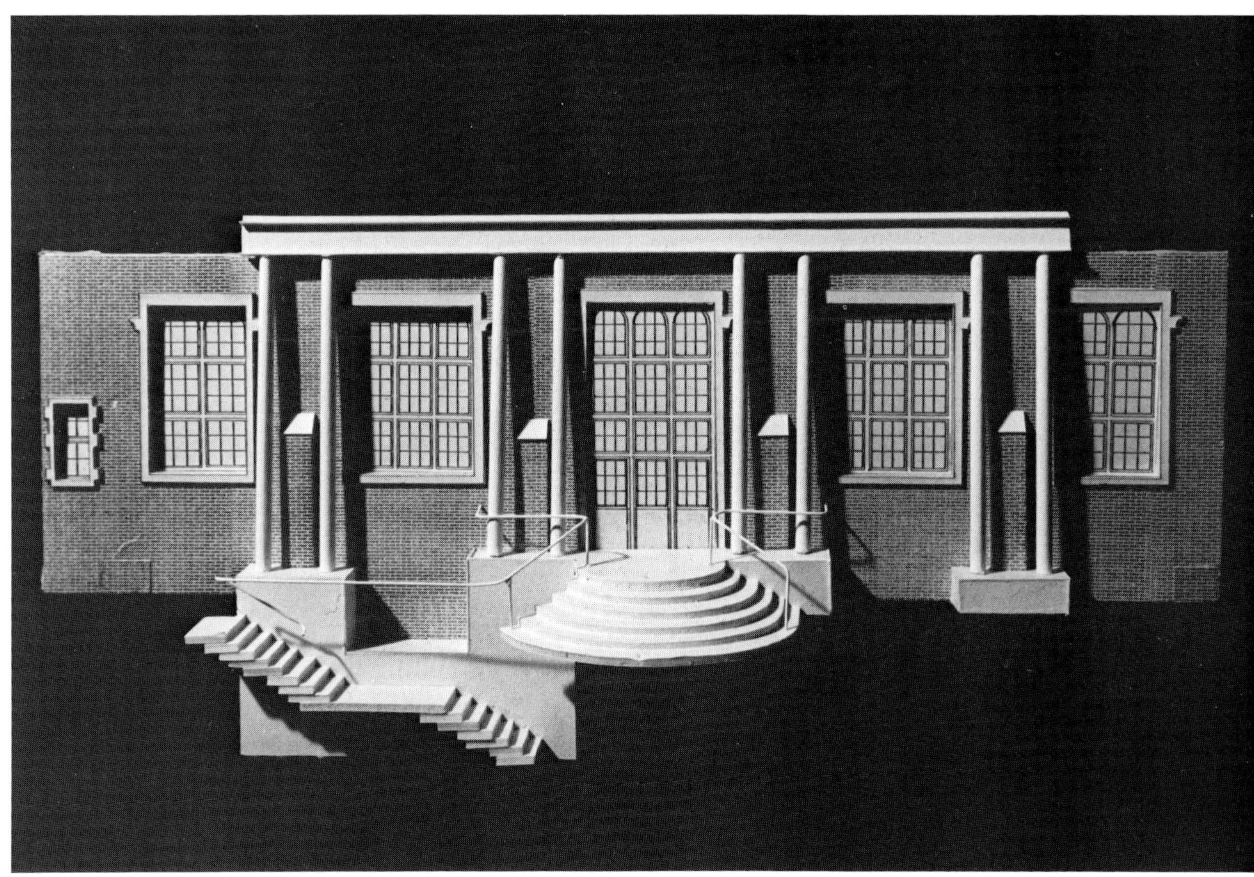

Figure 6.6
An addition of a stairway and colonnade to an existing facade was studied and presented in the form of a component model.

BEHAVIORAL MODELING

Beyond the simple massing of forms, modeling techniques can be used to introduce more complex factors in the design process. In the earlier stages, composite, three-dimensional arrangements can be assembled using card and paper to depict such factors as environmental conditions, site implications, user requirements, and other elements that are less tangible than walls and windows but are likely to be important constraints upon the final design.

When the model is kept abstract, most important variables in the design process can be introduced. Color, drawn images, and writing may also be included for the designer's benefit, so that the final product is literally a three-dimensional brief. From this, the designer can proceed to formalize the design into more conventional model forms, translating the information into architectural elements which are compatible with the variables originally highlighted. This technique enables the designer to take information from a wide range of sources at various levels of abstraction and to incorporate it into a comprehensive image corresponding to the visual nature of design. Such an exercise would be more difficult if the data were contained in a written or other nonvisual format.

Behavioral modeling may be useful in designs which involve participation by nondesigners, who can provide input to the design process without needing any drawing or design skills.

Figure 6.7
Behavioral modeling can be very effective in demonstrating a variety of variables which should be taken into consideration during the design phase. The impermanent nature of the model means that a range of papers and cards, some heavily annotated, can be employed.

SIMULATION MODELING

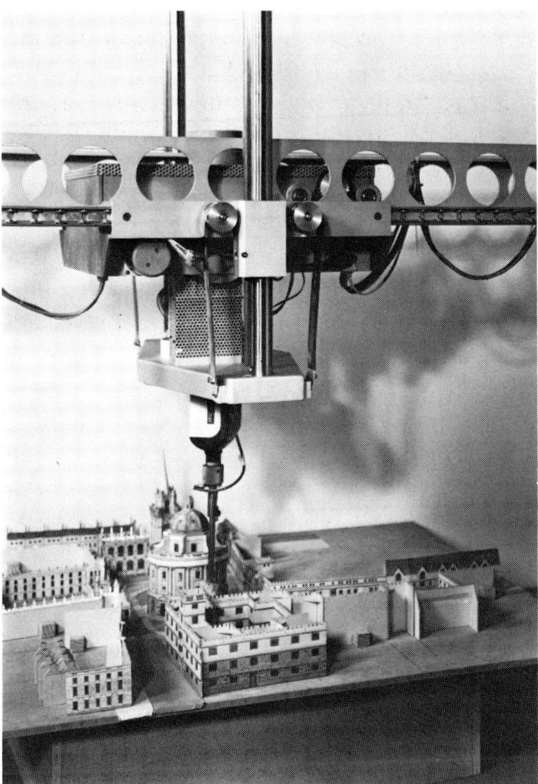

Figure 6.8
Urban spaces can be effectively and realistically explored using relatively basic equipment and simple models.

As representations of spatial quality, models can be taken to a further degree of completion and, with the use of additional equipment, can be used to show designed space from a relatively realistic perspective. The modelscope, for example, is a useful tool for exploring a model from within. The device resembles a small periscope through which the viewer can penetrate areas of the model where the human head could not fit, obtaining a realistic impression of the space at roughly scaled proportions. The modelscope can be used with interior or site models, and it can be attached to a camera to produce photographs or slides of the spaces for further presentation or analysis.

A more sophisticated method of simulating a spatial experience utilizes a video camera system, where the lens is literally driven through a constructed model of, for example, street layouts and transmits the images onto a television screen. The process can generate some remarkably realistic eye-level images, but for convincing results it does require a simulator and a reasonably high quality of finish.

If spatial representation is taken to its logical conclusion, it would seem reasonable to use full-sized mockups of forms and spaces so that the actual implications of the design can be judged. These may often be too difficult to prepare, although the mockup of I. M. Pei's proposed gallery addition to the Louvre in Paris shows how simple cables stretched to describe the outline of an intended form can reveal much about a building without resorting to many complex construction procedures.

DETAIL

In model building, there is always a question as to how much detail should be included. Models in the design phase, for example, are intended solely to enable the designer to explore and modify form decisions quickly and easily. Consequently, the techniques employed should not be either time-consuming or aimed at producing finished-looking work, which the designer may be reluctant to change further. Accordingly, simple techniques involving card and tape or fast-setting glue or foam-cored card and pins should be used for maximum effect.

In the presentation process, some designers take a minimal or rudimentary approach to model building, allowing accompanying drawings to convey the more detailed aspects of the scheme. Varying degrees of abstraction can be used, and some models may be little more than working forms generated during the design phase. At the other end of the scale, it is possible to include a very high level of detail, trying to emulate the features of the intended building as closely as possible. Attention to color, texture, and building and landscape details can produce a very effective

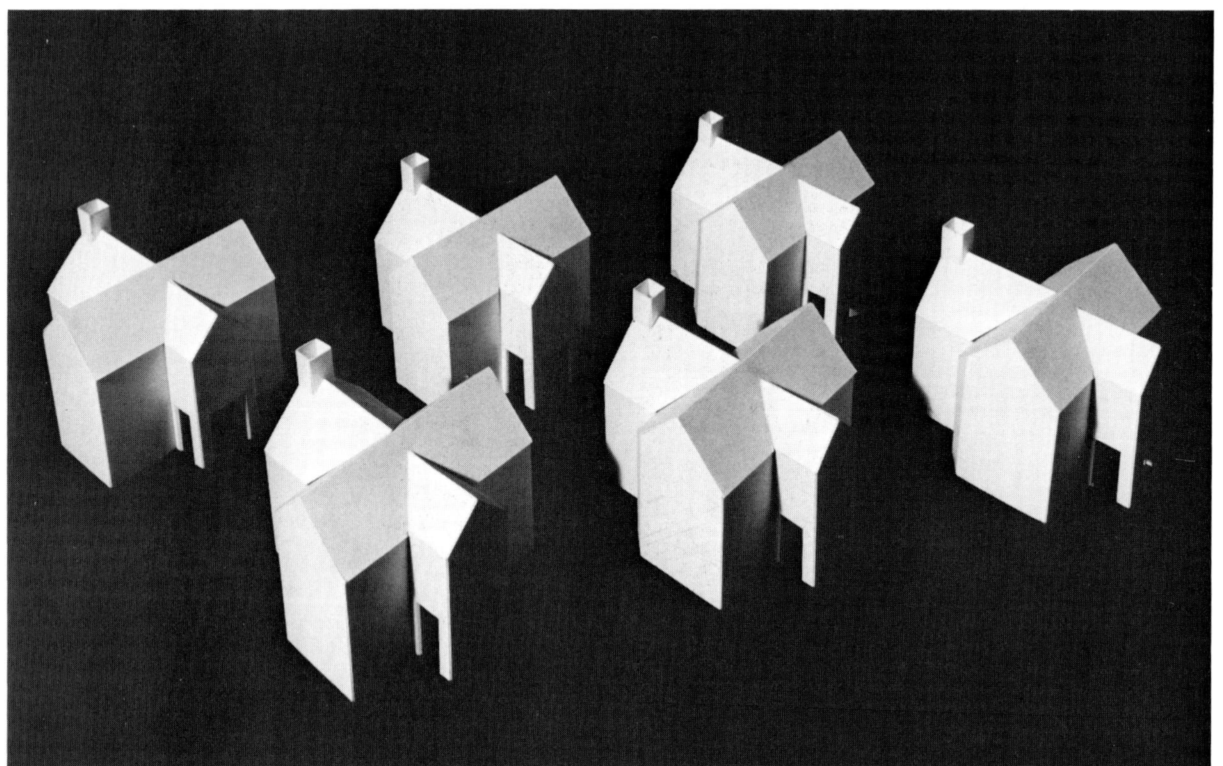

Figure 6.9
Once a single unit had been developed for a prototypical housing project, abstract massing models were built of white card in order to experiment with different site-planning configurations, which were then recorded photographically. Since the models were used to study site planning and massing, they were built with little or no surface detail.

product, which can potentially be used in conjunction with photographic techniques. However, such models require a high level of skill in their completion. Models which aim at a level of sophisticated finish but are inexpertly crafted tend to diminish the power of the presentation and are perhaps less effective than a simple form model which visually promises less.

Care must also be taken with the issue of scale. Representation of color, texture, and building elements such as bricks and windows at a fraction of the original size can present problems of construction and realism. The subtlety necessary in scaling down the tone and detail of model elements is sometimes forgotten, and many models, by attempting to be realistic, appear instead brightly colored or overdone.

Although most models are constructed of simple cardboard and glue, there are certain alternatives which can provide interesting results, particularly in the presentation process. Some fine models have been constructed, for example, by using strathmore paper which can be formed into precise, monochromatic

Figure 6.10
This model of urban townhouses was constructed of chipboard but carefully assembled and embellished with lichen (plants), basswood (window and door frames), and plastic-covered wire (handrails).

forms. Similarly, other thin materials can be used to "coat" forms created from cardboard. This technique may be useful in covering up sloppy construction or in adding a level of texture and/or color to the model. In this way, a design process model can be revamped for presentation purposes. Extra information such as materials or windows can also be added by drawing directly on the applied surface before sticking it to the base model. A variation of this technique involves drawing the facade information onto tracing paper, printing it, and pasting it to the model. The original drawing can then still be used in the presentation drawings. Similarly, reproductions of existing images (photographs or drawings of brickwork, for example) can be pasted to the model surface to provide a realistic impression of the materials in question.

The finished model, besides being useful as a presentation device, can be used as a vehicle for some sophisticated drawing techniques

Figure 6.11
Stiff white strathmore paper was used to create the model, which is monochromatic and articulated only to the thickness of the paper at the apertures. The effect is stylishly sculptural.

utilizing photography. Images of the model (potentially taken using a modelscope) can be incorporated into the final presentation in either print or slide format. The photographs also can be used as a base for sketching perspective views of the design. As a means of generating a series of fast perspectives, a simple form model can provide virtually limitless shots of the design, which can be traced, and to which can be added a further level of drawn detail. This process saves time both in the construction of the model (which need be only rudimentary if the detail can be added in drawing form) and in the laborious construction of a series of perspectives.

A further refinement to this technique requires the taking of black and white photographs of a simple, monochromatic form model, which are then photocopied. The designer can add detail and color to these images and incorporate them into the final design.

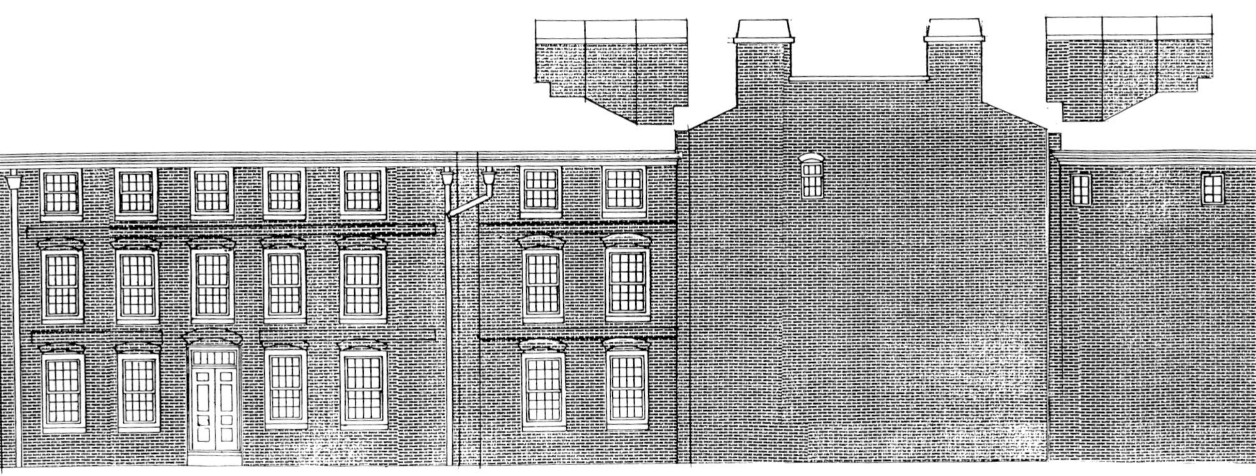

Figure 6.12
In order to create a highly detailed model of an eighteenth-century Boston townhouse, photocopied windows, doors, downspouts, and moldings were cut and pasted onto a sheet of brick texture. The completed elevations were then pasted onto a sheet of board, cut out, and folded into a massing model, to which only the roof and parapet cap were added.

Figures 6.13–6.14
A simple massing model of a housing project was built and then photographed with color slide film. From these slides, color photocopies were made, and all architectural details (such as trellis-work, windows, textures, and trees) were drawn in using colored pencil to produce a realistic perspective drawing.

DURABILITY AND LONGEVITY

If the model is to be viewed only on a single occasion, it should be viewed as temporary in nature and constructed accordingly. Materials such as foam core board or card can be used to produce fast, effective models, although they may deteriorate quickly. If a record of the model is desirable, it should be photographed as soon as possible after completion. However, if the final product is intended for long-term display or storage, it may be advisable to use materials and techniques that will not buckle, unstick, fade, or deteriorate over time. Perhaps the best high-quality finish can be obtained by using basswood. The final product is virtually indestructible, looks very elegant, and even tends to age well as the wood seasons.

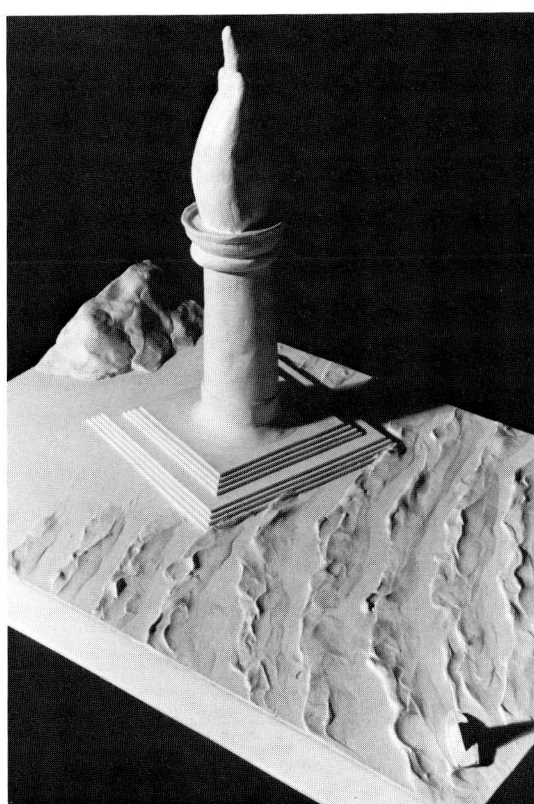

Figure 6.15 (at left)
This model of a liberty monument was built of both board (the base and steps) and clay (the waves, tower, and lantern). The entire model was then painted white to unify the surfaces and photographed to produce perspective drawings. See Figure 4.2.

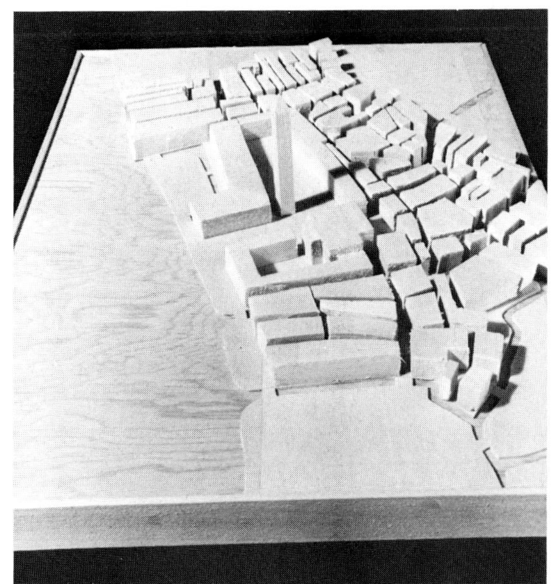

Figure 6.16 (at right)
This study model of a section of Venice was built of basswood blocks with no surface detail. Like a figure ground drawing, this model describes built solids in relation to unbuilt voids.

Figure 6.17
The high-quality finish of this hardwood model will not diminish with age, will withstand a reasonable amount of rough treatment, and will actually "mellow" as the wood ages.

Chapter Seven
Presentation Techniques

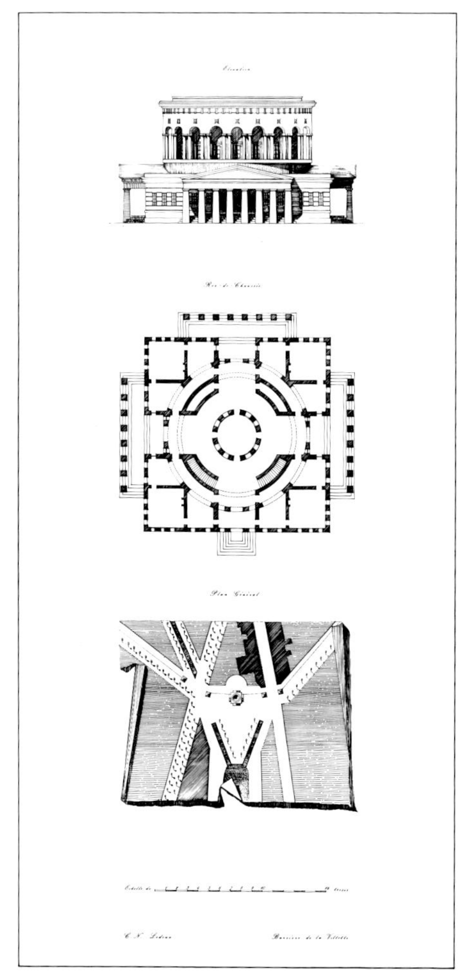

Although the presentation of a project is in itself secondary to the actual design, the importance of appropriate communication should not be underrated or ill-conceived. Considering the number of hours that a designer will put into the design process, it is shortsighted to either inadequately or badly present the final ideas to the intended audience, who may either not fully understand the designer's intent or be unimpressed by the poor visual display. Consequently, it is important to consider and plan the presentation as early as possible, preferably in the earliest phases of the design. In this way, the presentation process can be seen as a continuation of the design process rather than a separate and distinct function, and work can be arranged in such a way as to facilitate and abbreviate the procedures.

Targeting the Audience

It is first necessary to establish a clear profile of the intended audience and tailor the presentation accordingly. For example, a general lay audience may need far more explanatory data than a panel of experts, who may be presented with relatively sophisticated or complex information. The presentor should also bear in mind the method of presentation. If he or she will be present to orally supplement a visual display, questions or misunderstandings can be easily handled. If the work is to be evaluated without the benefit of verbal assistance, it must rely totally on the content of the presentation for clarity of communication.

Focusing the Presentation

The purpose for making the presentation should be evaluated, and the desired outcome determined. It may be the intention of the presentor to impress or persuade the target audience as to the viability of a design. Alternatively, the designer may want to explain some basic concepts to a decision-making audience to ascertain their reaction or to extract some information or instructions from them, particularly at initial or interim meetings.

The desired outcome of the meeting will therefore affect the type of media used. Where the designer is seeking to create an impression, the graphics are likely to be highly crafted and complete, whereas presentations designed to stimulate discussion or a flow of information are likely to appear more open-ended and informational in content. In the latter case, quick, effective graphic techniques are likely to be the most appropriate, suggesting a capacity for further changes in the design which may be precluded by highly crafted drawings.

Previous chapters have sought to explore the range, applicability, and use of potential drawing types and graphic techniques that can be used in the design and presentation processes, but as yet we have not considered their composite, overall impact. This concluding chapter therefore discusses the final production of the design and the means by which the ultimate display of work can be assembled for the most effective results.

Developing the Presentation

Although presentation has been dealt with here primarily as a graphic phenomenon, there are obviously alternative applications which can be utilized in the communication of design ideas. Good presentation planning involves the consideration of all available means—graphic, verbal, written, and visual—and enables the designer to develop a mix appropriate to the project and means of display. Careful selection at this stage can ensure that unnecessary duplication (where the same information is produced in several formats) is avoided and that the overall mix of media communicates the scheme to the best advantage. Where the duplication of work *is* desirable, however—for example, in the simultaneous preparation of a wall display and a report, or in the preparation of a model for display and photographic exploration—careful planning in terms of size, proportion, and method of reproducibility can save time and effort later in the presentation process.

Written Presentations

In many cases, the power of the written word is likely to be necessary to supplement or even supplant graphic images, as, for example, in press releases. Information on drawings can convey conceptual or technical detail not compatible to graphic illustration or can clarify and embellish drawings to ease the process of communication. Handouts, booklets, and reports are also likely to require a clear, unambiguous written component, and designers should not seek to rely entirely upon the power of drawing to communicate ideas. In any presentation, the balance of visual and written material should be developed with the sole purpose of making the final product as clear and impressive as possible.

Verbal Presentations

In a jury situation, open meetings, or in discussions with clients, the designer has the added advantage of supplementing the graphic display with a verbal explanation, taking the audience through the scheme, clarifying any misunderstandings, and elaborating upon the advantages of the design. The style of verbal presentation will vary according to the audience and in all cases should be planned and rehearsed beforehand. Verbal presentations should be kept short and pertinent, making full use of the drawings and any associated media. Cue cards or a formal written outline may help the presentor, while in long, complex meetings, handouts may be useful to guide audiences through the scheme.

Visual Presentations

The majority of design-oriented presentations will involve visual display, although conventional drawings may be supplemented or even replaced by alternative media. Slide shows, for example, can be very effective in illustrating information, and have a flexibility in mix which is hard to achieve in drawings. Site information, written data, design drawings, and models can all be brought together into a coherent, consistent presentation format. Models can be photographed either at eye level or with a modelscope to produce realistic visions of the scheme. Similarly, the video camera can be used to great effect in generating realistic images and can be particularly effective in exploring large-scale models, as detailed in Chapter 6. When using technical media either individually or in conjunction with a visual display, it is important to ensure that the location of the presentation has adequate blackout and screening facilities, and that there is a convenient power supply.

Graphic Presentations

Traditional layouts, particularly where clarity of communication is the primary issue (as in, for example, working drawings), tend to have the individual drawings arranged in a logical sequence, where plans are stacked and elevations and sections grouped. As general presentation drawings, however, they may appear technical and uninspiring, particularly if large areas of white space detract from the individual images and overall sheet impact.

Each sheet should be carefully planned and laid out to maximize the use of the background and the interrelationship of the individual images. This may be handled in a logical or ordered manner, or the designer may attempt to integrate the individual images into a fluid, comprehensive entity by interweaving or fusing them together. Care should be taken in the latter case to prevent visual confusion from overwhelming the completed drawing.

Information, whether presented on a single or series of sheets, may be ordered to create different emphases. For example, logical layouts of material may lead the viewer along a linear progression of work, so that the information is approached in the intended sequence and no material is omitted from view. This may be particularly useful in situations where the designer has little or no opportunity to explain the drawings, and the presentation must speak for itself (as, for example, in the case of competition entries).

If emphasis is required, either on an individual drawing or on a specific concept that is intended to be an audience focus, the presentation may be arranged hierarchically in both scale and graphic impact.

For particular emphasis, the presentation may be arranged to emulate the character of the design being represented. For example, a thematic display may help to reinforce the intent of the design, although some care should be taken to prevent the overall package from becoming overly exaggerated or tasteless. More atmospheric schemes may take other thematic approaches, subordinating the individual graphics to the overall image of the display. Again, this technique can be very effective in attracting an audience's attention, but it should be tempered with caution to prevent the presentation from appearing frivolous.

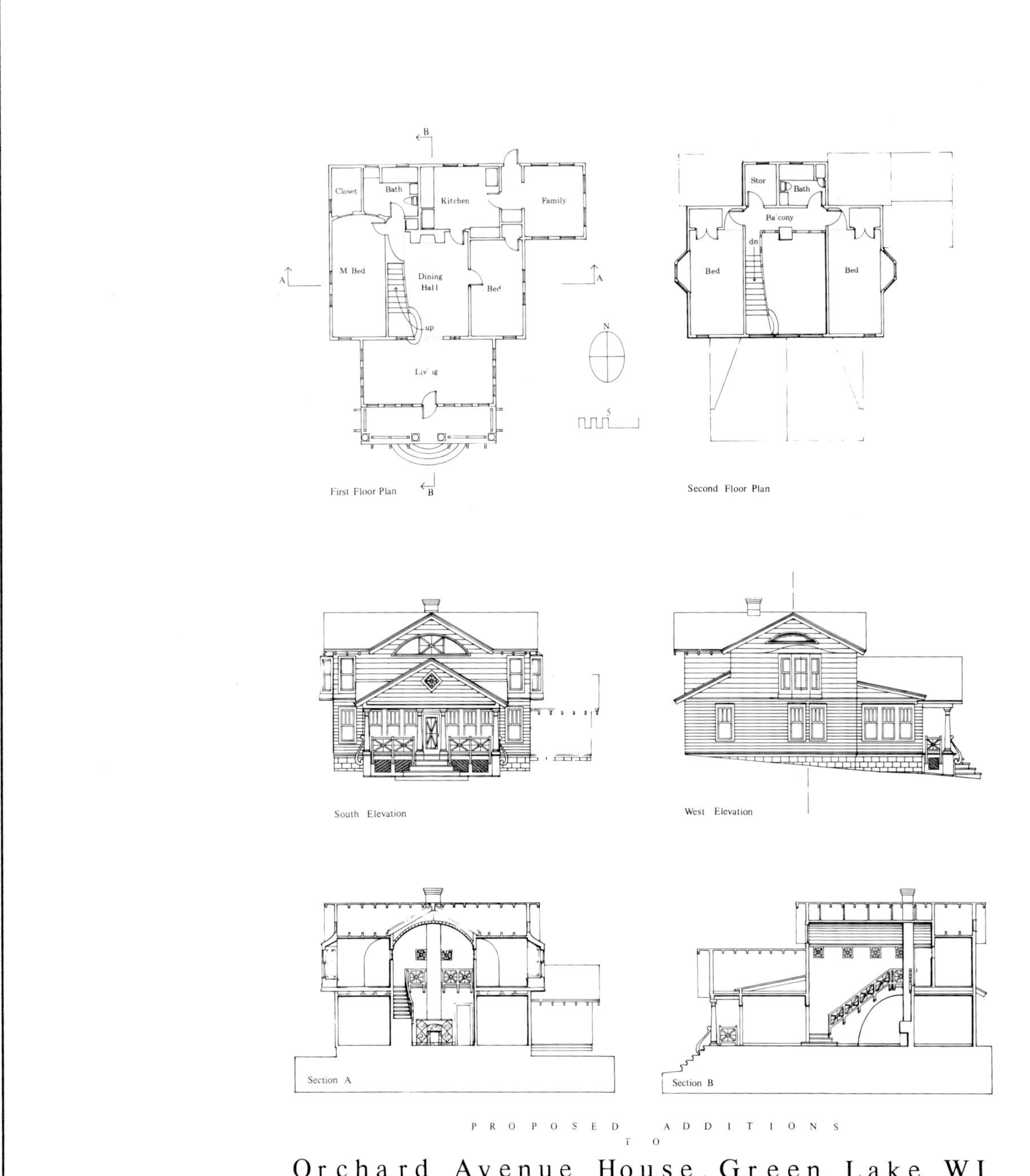

Figure 7.1
The individual drawings for a proposed addition to a house are laid out in a regular, conventional manner on the sheet.

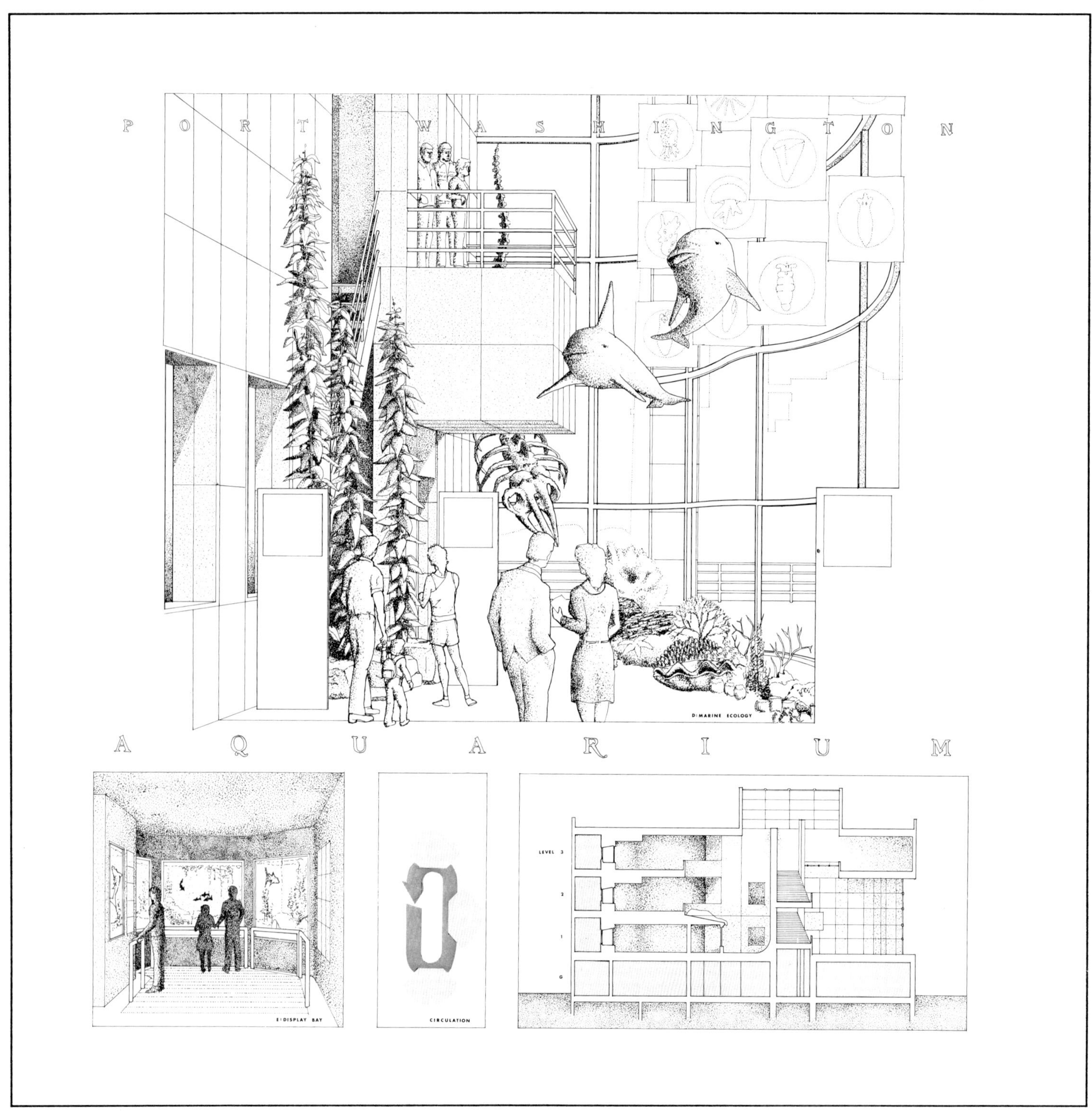

Figures 7.2–7.3
Design ideas for an aquarium are displayed on the two sheets. Each board contains a variety of ideas and drawing types which could have resulted in visual chaos. However, they are both laid out with a hierarchically strong central image which provides focus, allowing the smaller images to cluster around the perimeter.

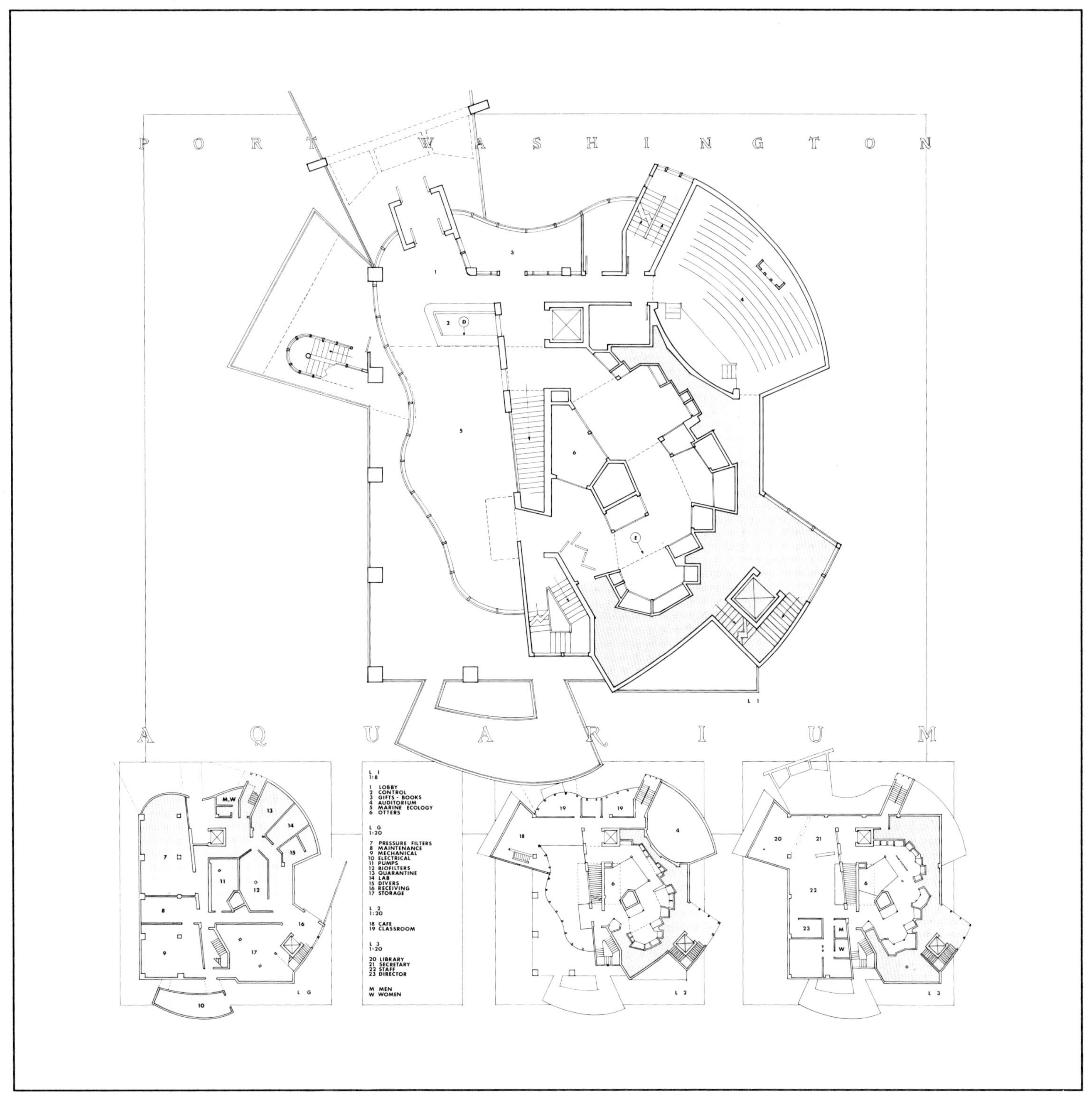
PORT WASHINGTON
AQUARIUM
L 1
1:8
1 LOBBY
2 CONTROL
3 GIFTS - BOOKS
4 AUDITORIUM
5 MARINE ECOLOGY
6 OTTERS
L G
1:20
7 PRESSURE FILTERS
8 MAINTENANCE
9 MECHANICAL
10 ELECTRICAL
11 PUMPS
12 BIOFILTERS
13 QUARANTINE
14 LAB
15 DIVERS
16 RECEIVING
17 STORAGE
L 2
1:20
18 CAFE
19 CLASSROOM
L 3
1:20
20 LIBRARY
21 SECRETARY
22 STAFF
23 DIRECTOR
M MEN
W WOMEN
L 1
L G
L 2
L 3

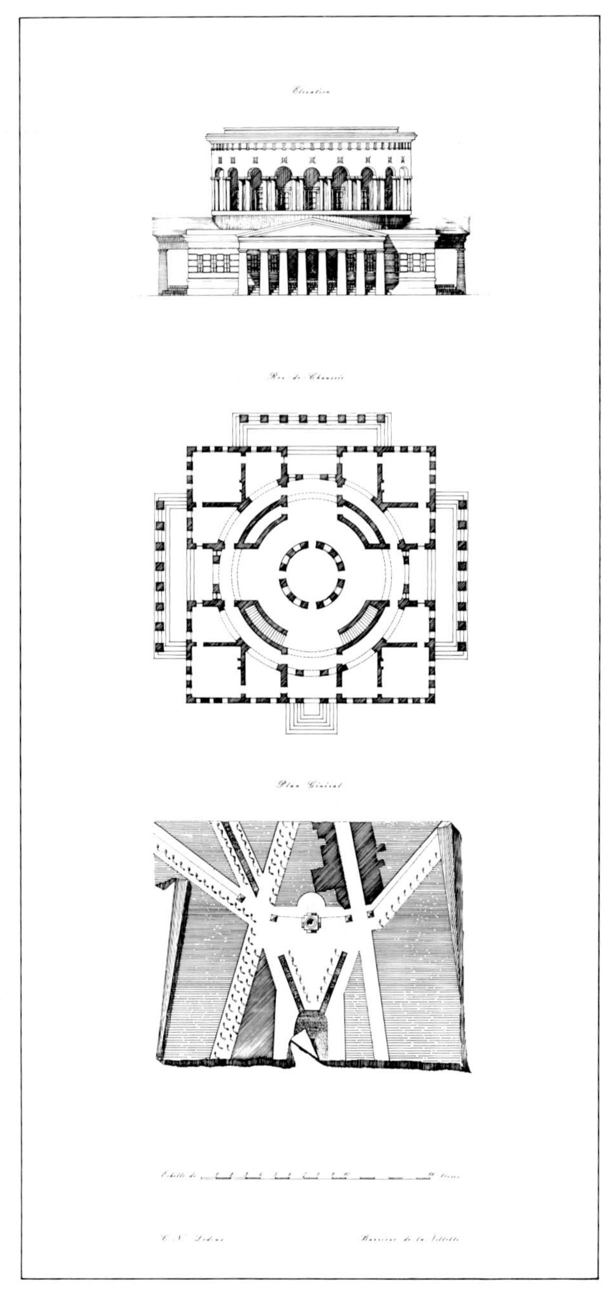

Figure 7.4
This drawing for Ledoux's Paris gateway shows a simple axial relationship between the plan and elevation, giving the site plan a certain prominence on a graphically "separate" sheet.

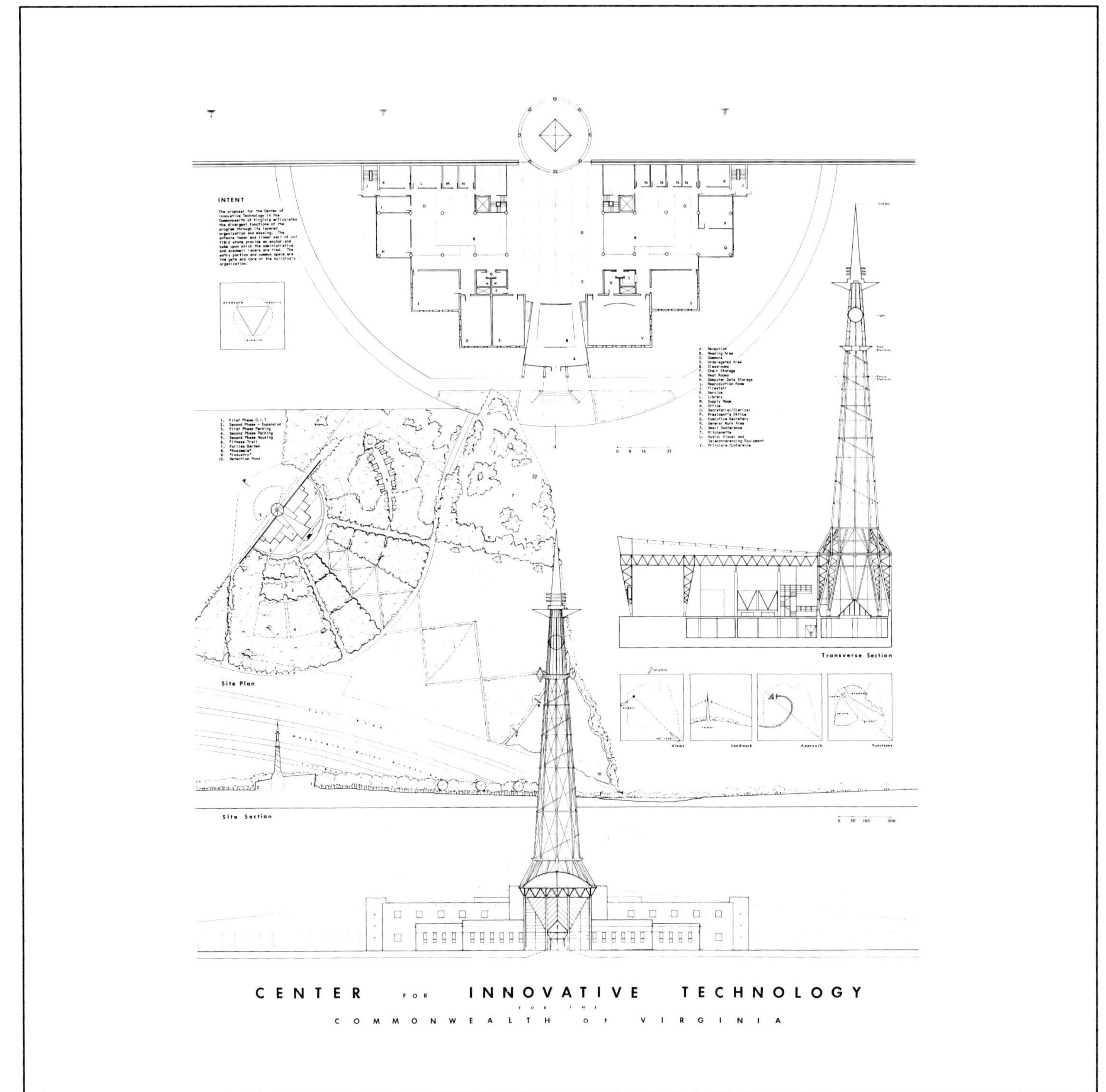

Figure 7.5
The integration of drawings on the sheet provides a powerful graphic image without confusion, owing to the careful hierarchical positioning of the various elements and the high quality of graphic presentation.

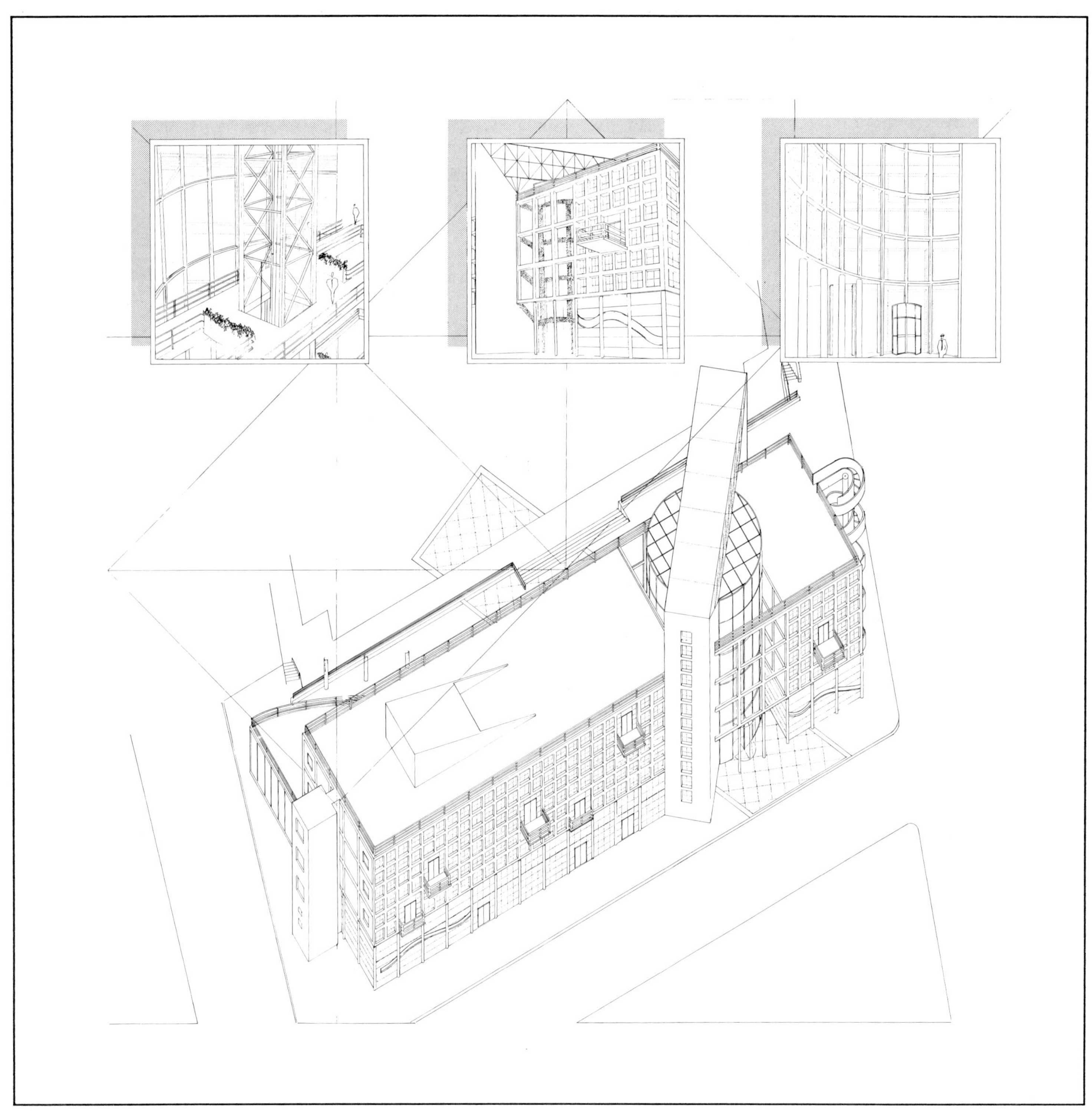

Figure 7.6
The use of graphic gridwork on the sheet helps to integrate the images and create a powerful overall image.

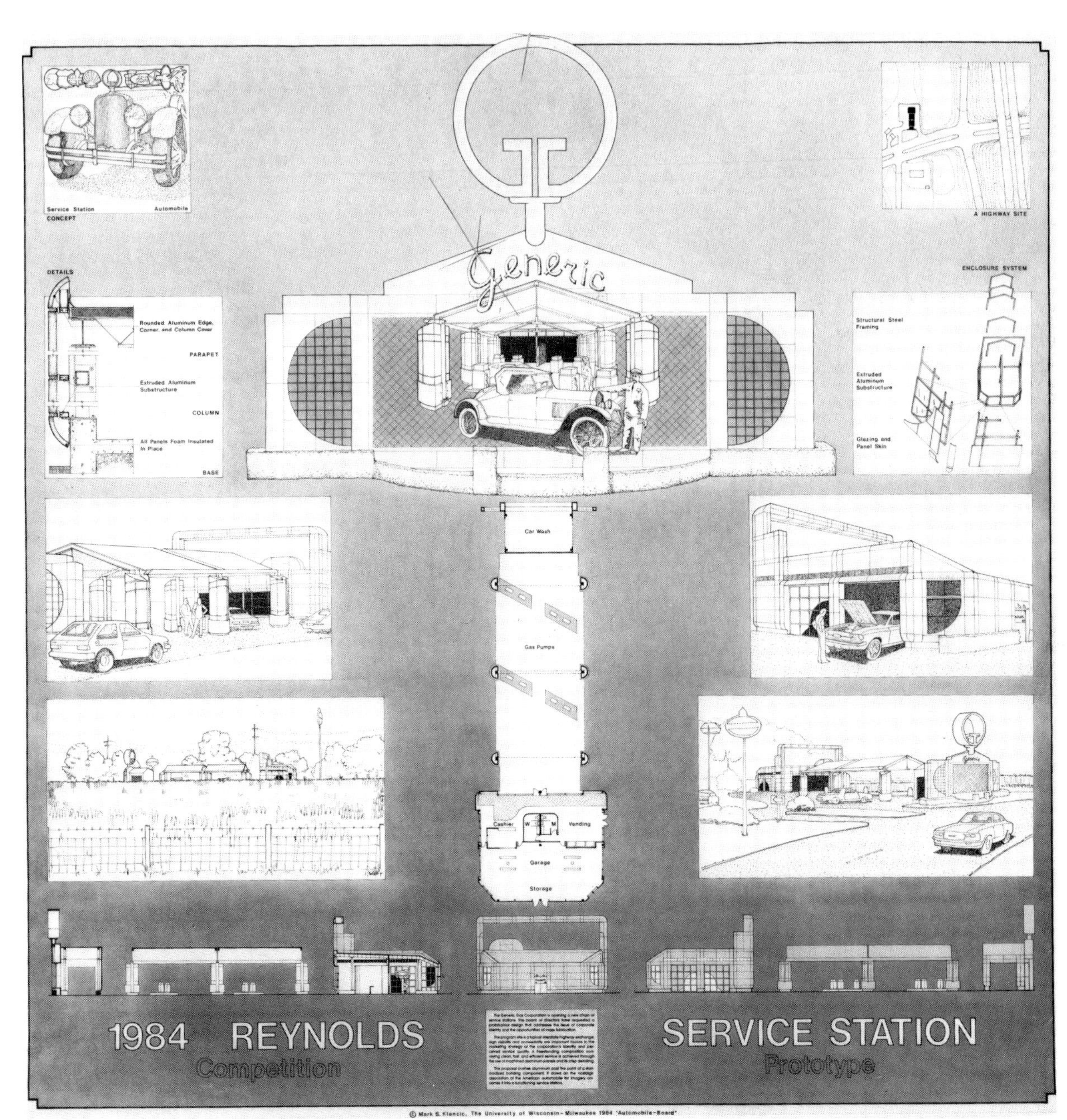

Figure 7.7
This award-winning competition entry utilizes the theme of an automobile in the design of a garage and reflects the flavor of the scheme in the presentation format.

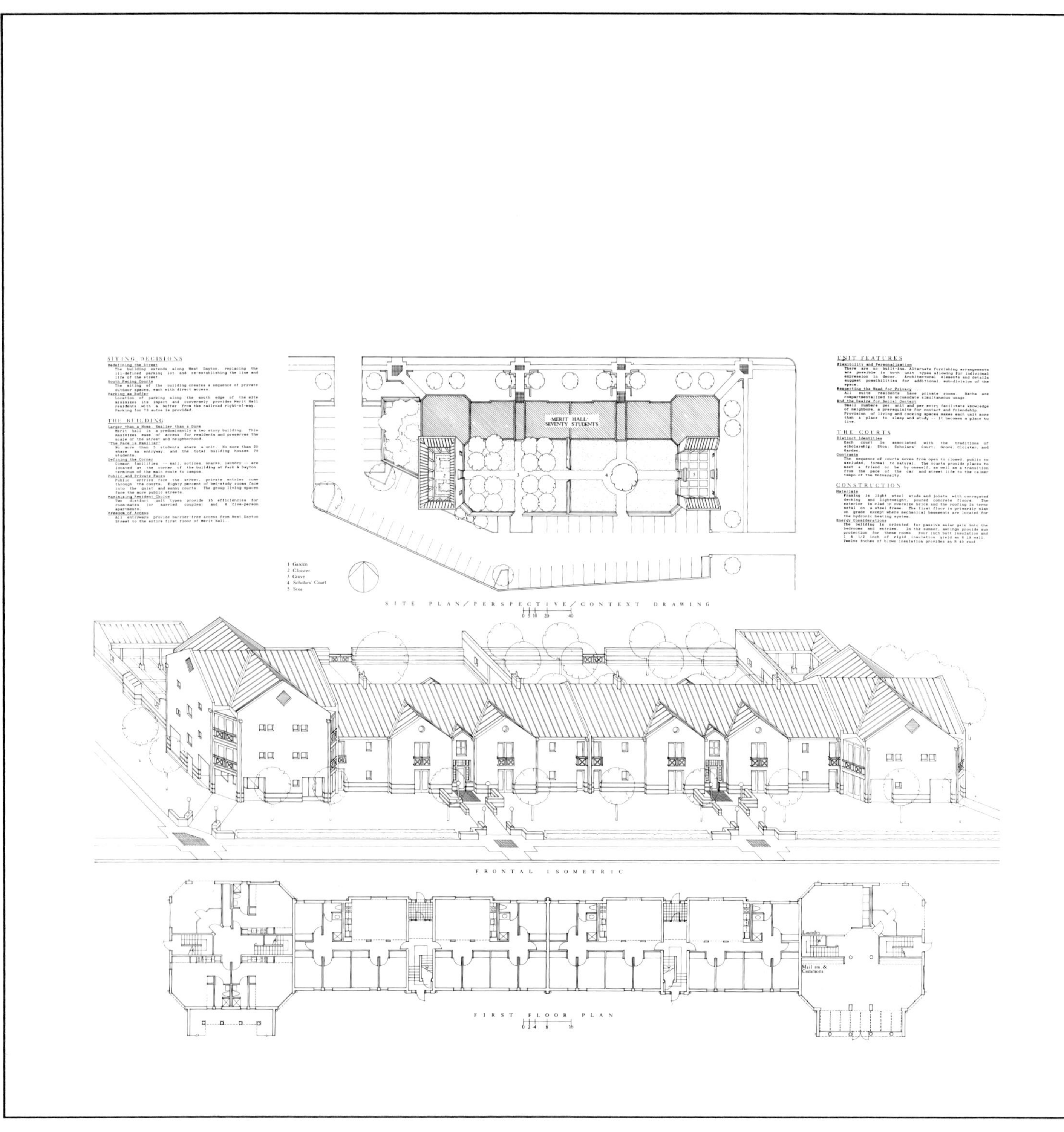

Figures 7.8–7.9
Detailed information concerning costs formed part of the presentation for the winning entry in a competition for the design of a dormitory building. Similar information, such as conceptual strategies or circulation routes, for example, may not be particularly graphic but may give the viewer a clearer idea of the nature of the project.

COSTS

The cost data were provided by Dodge Conceptual Budget Analysis for a building of the specified construction and insulation in the configuration shown. Costs for 23 kitchen units and 23 baths are included in these figures as well. The data are based upon costs in Madison, Wisconsin with construction beginning in March 1985. The economical building design proposed will thus free a portion of the total budget for development of the courts, gardens and walls. While these are not inexpensive items, we believe that they contribute substantially to the overall project and are at the core of collegiate architecture and engender the spirit of scholarship.

STONE RESIDENCE
MADISON WISCONSIN

SEPTEMBER 16, 1984 ESTIMATE NO. 1005

DESCRIPTION	LABOR	MATERIAL	TOTAL	SQ FT
FOUNDATIONS	19,791	12,222	32,013	2.00
FLOORS ON GRADE	10,372	11,544	21,916	1.36
SUPERSTRUCTURES	26,036	56,904	82,940	5.18
ROOFING	9,853	11,387	21,240	1.33
EXTERIOR WALLS	106,474	81,571	188,045	11.75
PARTITIONS	31,721	49,812	81,533	5.09
WALL FINISHES	23,509	11,786	35,295	2.20
FLOOR FINISHES	10,620	4,564	15,184	0.94
CEILING FINISHES	18,915	9,180	28,095	1.75
FIXED EQUIPMENT	22,379	54,200	76,579	4.78
HVAC	27,199	37,060	64,259	4.01
PLUMBING	26,107	38,125	64,232	4.01
ELECTRICAL	13,859	12,410	26,269	1.64
CONSTRUCTION TOTAL	346,715	390,845	737,560	46.[illegible]

Figure 7.10
This beautifully rendered analysis drawing is composed equally of text and graphic images and provides an enormous amount of information with a high level of graphic impact.

Figure 7.11
The scheme for the design of a railway station which won an award in a student competition was introduced by this carefully rendered perspective, giving the scheme a memorable focus.

Model Integration

Some presentations will include three-dimensional images to supplement the drawings. Often, models will be displayed on a separate table or surface, although there is no reason why they cannot be incorporated into a vertical display format if the compositional order of the presentation has a high priority. Alternatively, some may feel that the vertical nature of the form which has become a three-dimensional roof/site plan underutilizes the model and may wish to incorporate it on a horizontal base instead. For greater integration and conformity of the images, of course, photographs of the model may be used instead and worked into the presentation as previously described.

Presentation Content

Conventional drawing types (plans, elevations, etc.) will usually form the basis of most design presentations, and the type and mix of drawings in the final display should be chosen to match the nature of the design and the audience. If the latter will be reviewing the work in the absence of the designer, as in the case of competition entries, it is important that the drawings be clear and self-explanatory. The addition of conceptual information to the display may therefore be desirable to explain to an audience the thoughts and decisions which led to the final configuration. Simple diagrams, limited text, and representative images may help to clarify organizational elements, conceptual bases, constraints, and requirements or may even be used to give an overview of more specific information which cannot be included in the drawings without overly complicating them (structure, H.V.A.C., etc.).

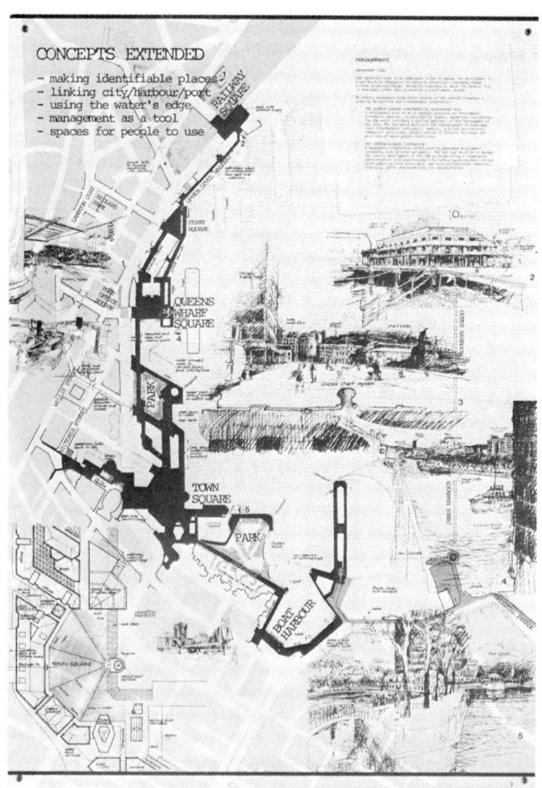

Figure 7.12
Part of the winning scheme in an international design competition, the sheet contains a variety of sketches, analytical plans, and conceptual statements which show the ideas behind the final solution.

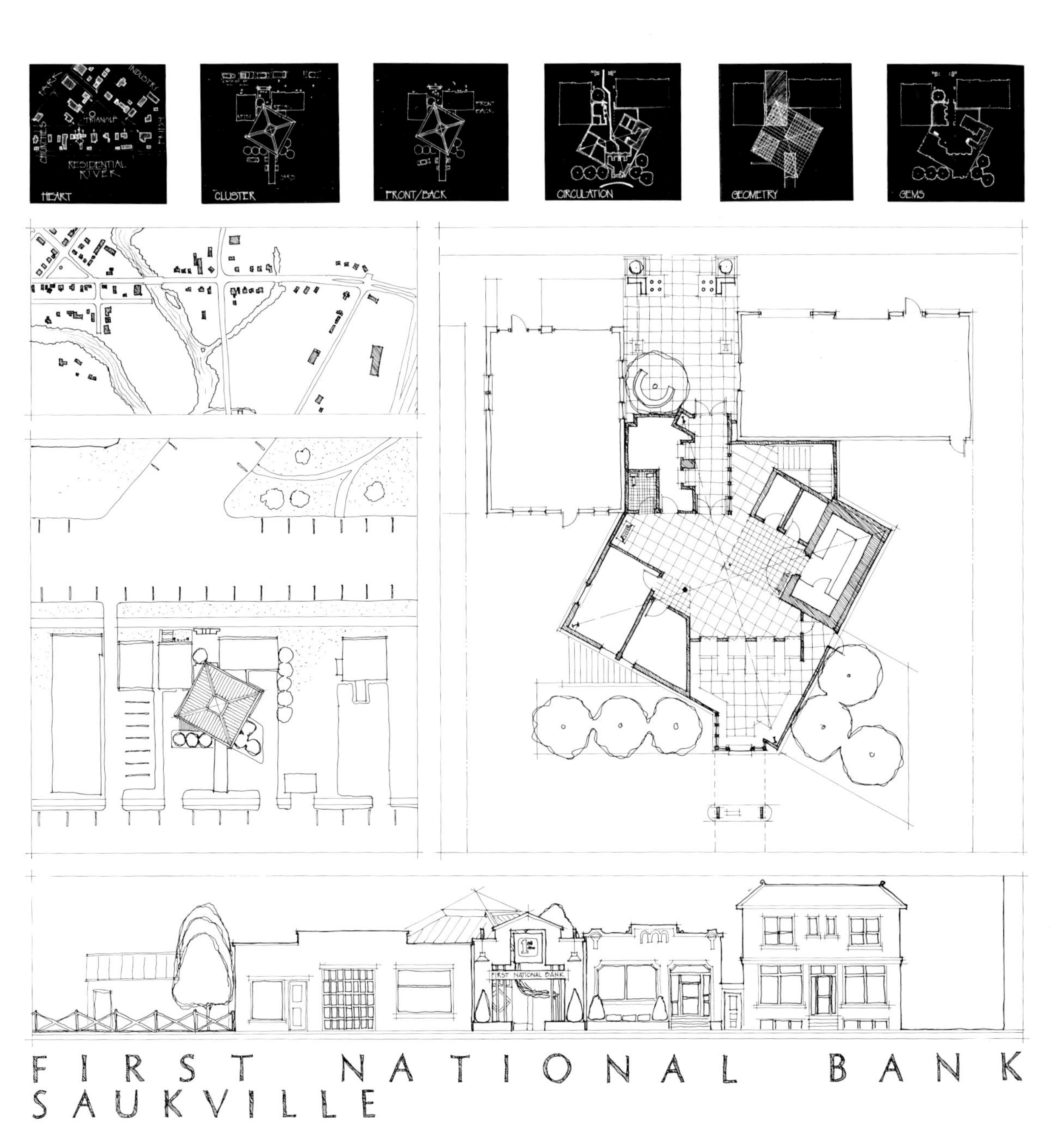

Figures 7.13–7.14
These two boards are carefully laid out to give some order to the varied images, but the images are drawn in a freehand manner to give a pleasantly casual style to the presentation. The small perspective drawings were generated by computer and then traced into the layout in the same style as the other images.

FIRST NATIONAL BANK
OF PORT WASHINGTON
WISCONSIN

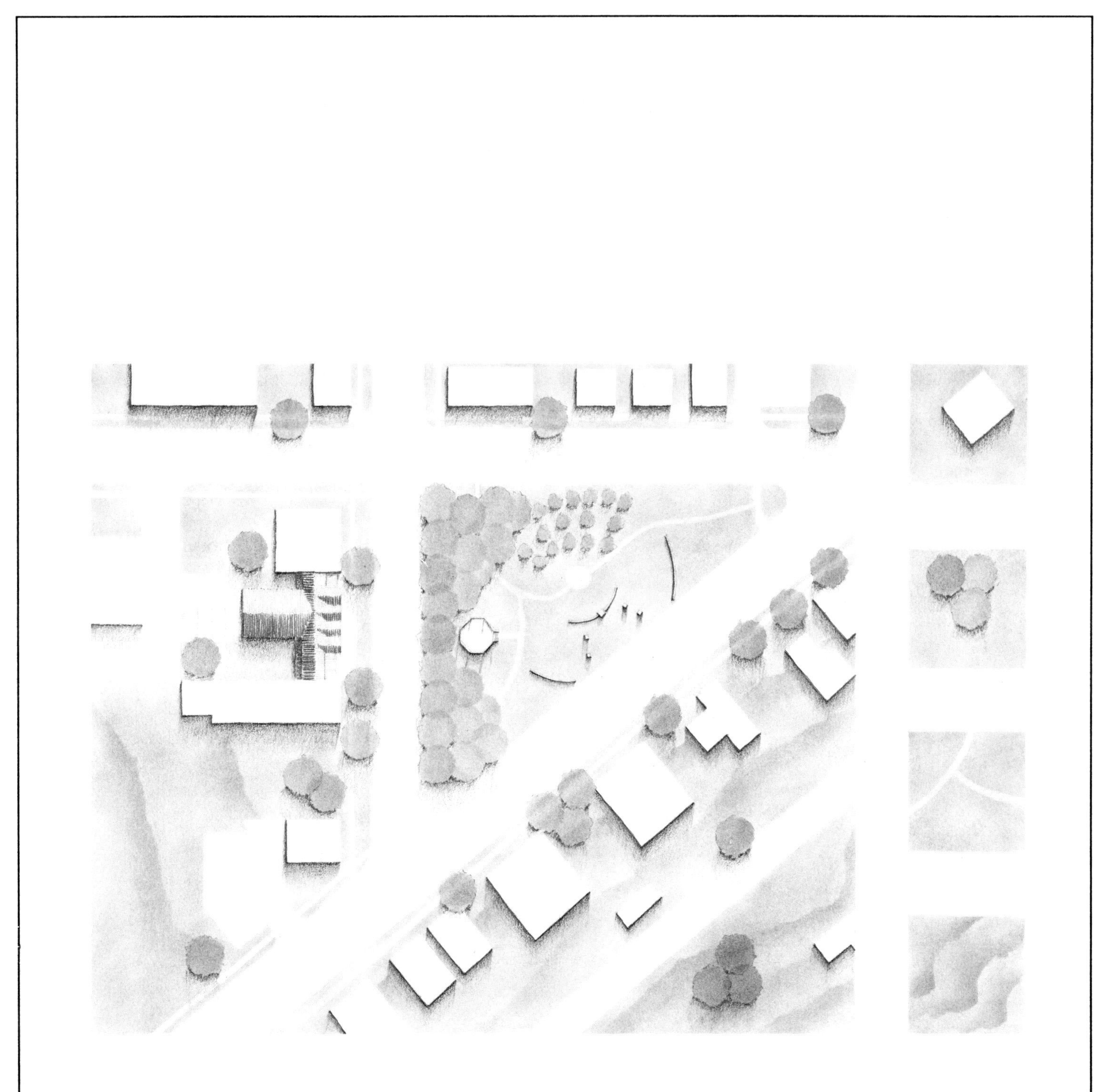

Figure 7.15
Some exciting presentation techniques can be generated by experimentation. This design for a small park was completed by carefully masking out areas of the sheet and applying powdered graphite with a tissue. Shading emphasis was added later using a soft pencil.

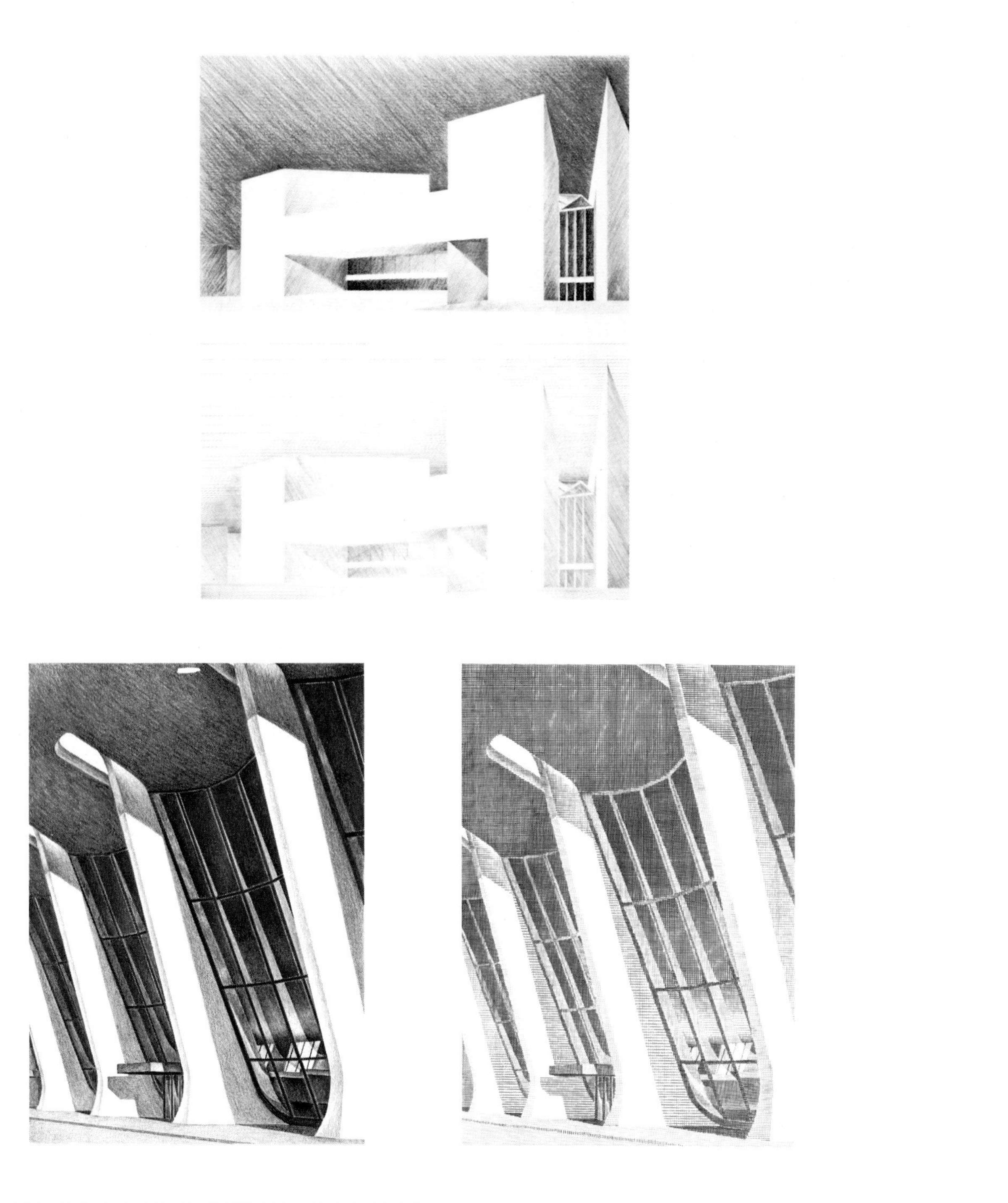

Figures 7.16–7.17
Presentation technique can radically affect the graphic impact or "flavor" of a scheme. Utilizing the same media but changing the application from shade to hardline hatch affects the final impact of the drawing.

COMPUTERS IN THE DESIGN AND PRESENTATION PROCESSES

Resistance against the computer has often been based on its inflexibility as a fast, lucid design tool and on the unimpressive quality of its printout. Although in very basic systems these assertions may be accurate, recent developments in computer technology have led to some remarkably sophisticated equipment which allows the user to manipulate images with as much ease as a pencil or drawing pen. Innovations such as a hand-held "mouse" enable the user to draw freehand onto the screen, and recently developed graphic packages provide broad ranges of lettering, shading symbols, and the like to embellish drawings. The introduction of color in the process, particularly when combined with sophisticated graphics programs, enables the creation of realistic, effective images which are more than adequate as presentation vehicles to clients.

Of course, there are some drawbacks to computer usage, although—perhaps surprisingly—cost is not one of them. Sophisticated packages which allow the greatest freedom of graphic exploration and presentation are relatively accessible to large practices and institutions. Basic systems, alternatively, are still capable of quite complex tasks and are now within the price range of many designers. The major problems in computer application appear to be not only in the realm of client understanding, which has already been discussed, but perhaps more importantly in the field of user understanding. Although some remarkable techniques are available, they require a degree of skill commensurate with the sophistication of the computer system. Even simple two-dimensional modeling requires thorough training before the user is fully familiarized with the process, while three-dimensional computer-aided design techniques, particularly combined with advanced graphic packages, require a high level of expertise. Often, the user does not possess sufficient expertise to effectively maximize the computer's potential, so despite the current availability of computing techniques, accessibility by appropriately trained individuals may still restrict its use.

However, as the computer becomes more and more an integral part of the design office, familiarity with its use will inevitably increase. Many schools of architecture, for example, are now introducing computer-aided design into their curriculum as a fundamental part of the design studio experience, where students are coming to accept the computer as a facile, flexible design tool as basic to their work as the pencil.

Figures 7.18–7.21
Computer applications continue to become more sophisticated, enabling the designer to generate powerful and exciting images without recourse to paper and pencil. Innovations in this field will continue to allow for more and more developments in graphic presentations.

Plan and elevation trees
Distant trees

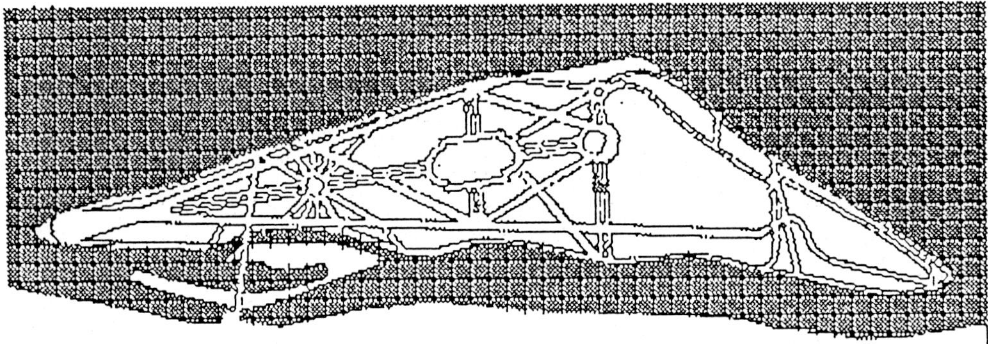

Plan View- Moulin Joli

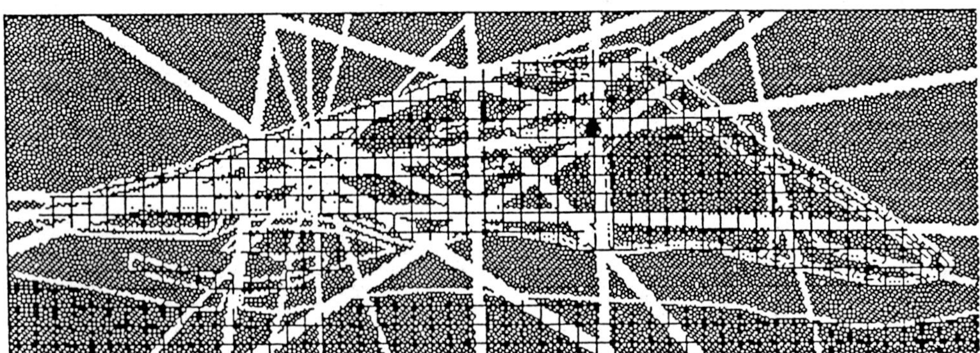

The Pattern of Paths

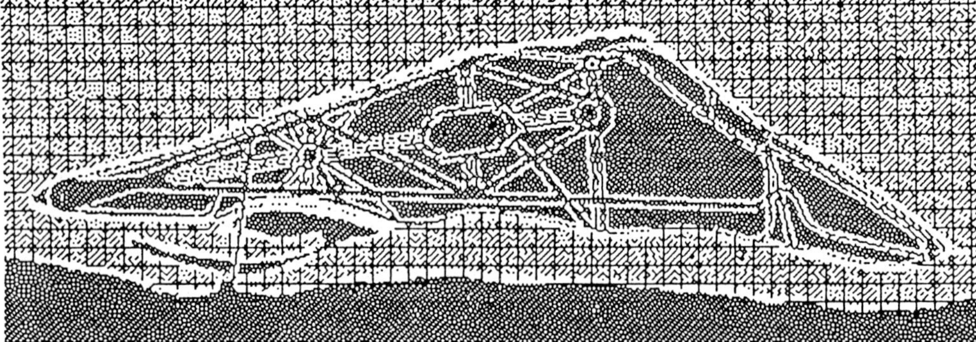

Plan View Again

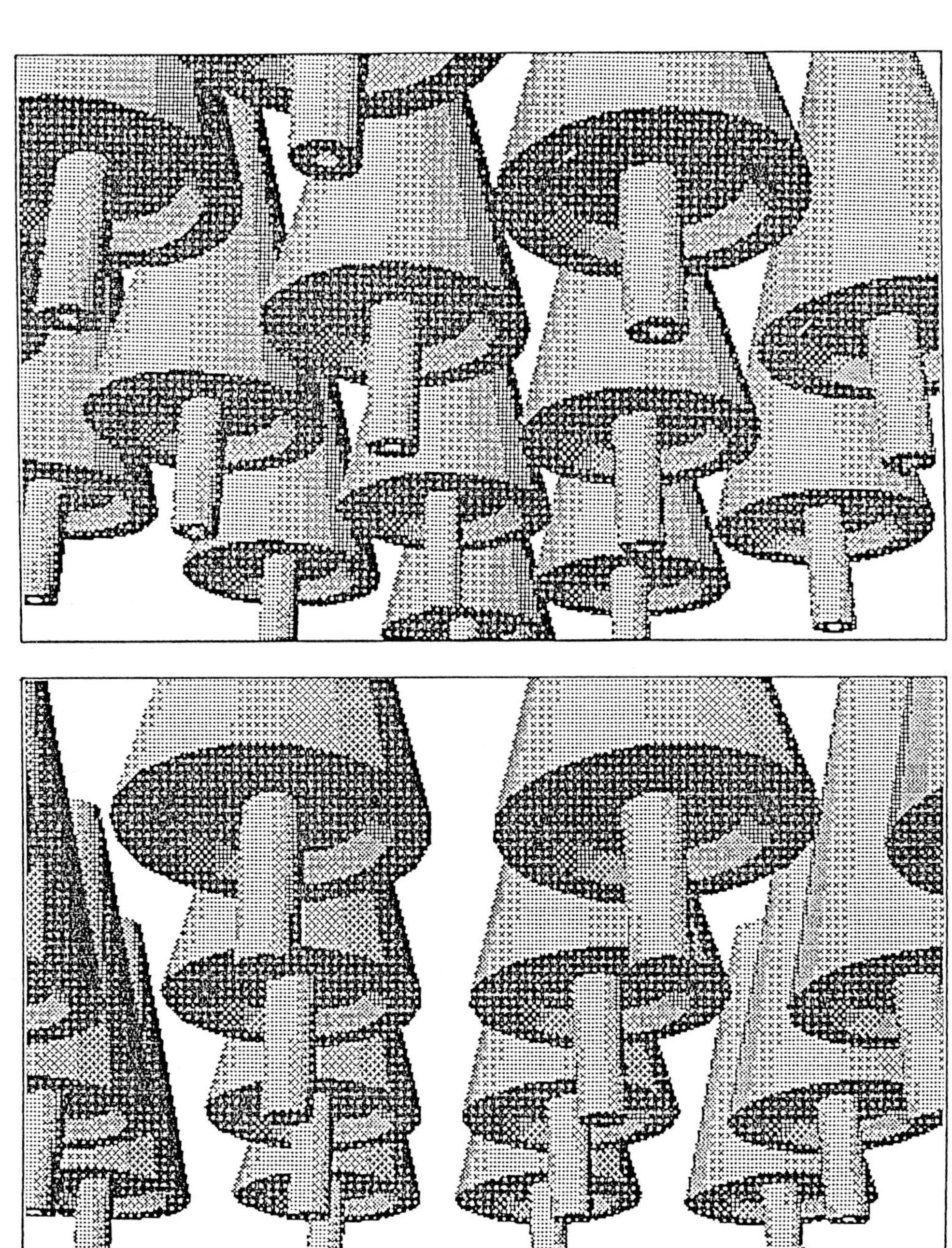

Index

O

P

R

S

T

U

V

W